PRISM

READING AND WRITING 1

Richard O'Neill

Michele Lewis

with
Wendy Asplin
Carolyn Flores

CAMBRIDGE
UNIVERSITY PRESS

CAMBRIDGE
UNIVERSITY PRESS

University Printing House, Cambridge CB2 8BS, United Kingdom

One Liberty Plaza, 20th Floor, New York, NY 10006, USA

477 Williamstown Road, Port Melbourne, VIC 3207, Australia

4843/24, 2nd Floor, Ansari Road, Daryaganj, Delhi – 110002, India

79 Anson Road, #06–04/06, Singapore 079906

Cambridge University Press is part of the University of Cambridge.

It furthers the University's mission by disseminating knowledge in the pursuit of education, learning and research at the highest international levels of excellence.

www.cambridge.org
Information on this title: www.cambridge.org/9781316624272

First published 2017

20 19 18 17 16 15 14 13 12 11 10 9 8 7 6 5 4 3 2 1

Printed in Dubai by Oriental Press

A catalogue record for this publication is available from the British Library

ISBN 978-1-316-62427-2 Student's Book with Online Workbook 1 Reading and Writing
ISBN 978-1-316-62508-8 Teacher's Manual 1 Reading and Writing

Cambridge University Press has no responsibility for the persistence or accuracy of URLs for external or third-party internet websites referred to in this publication, and does not guarantee that any content on such websites is, or will remain, accurate or appropriate. Information regarding prices, travel timetables, and other factual information given in this work is correct at the time of first printing but Cambridge University Press does not guarantee the accuracy of such information thereafter.

CONTENTS

SCOPE AND SEQUENCE

UNIT	WATCH AND LISTEN	READINGS	READING SKILLS	LANGUAGE DEVELOPMENT	
1 PLACES *Academic Disciplines* Sociology / Urban Planning	The Top U.S. City	1: Rise of the Megacities (article) 2: Homestay Vacations: A Home away from Home (article)	*Key Skill* Scanning for numbers *Additional Skills* Understanding key vocabulary Using your knowledge Reading for main ideas Reading for details Scanning to find information Scanning to predict content Working out meaning Making inferences Synthesizing	Nouns, verbs, and adjectives	
2 FESTIVALS AND CELEBRATIONS *Academic Disciplines* Anthropology / Cultural Studies	The Meaning of Independence Day	1: Celebrate! (article) 2: Muscat Festival (article)	*Key Skill* Previewing a text *Additional Skills* Understanding key vocabulary Scanning to predict content Reading for main ideas Reading for details Recognizing text type Synthesizing	Prepositions of time and place Adverbs of frequency	
3 THE INTERNET AND TECHNOLOGY *Academic Disciplines* Computer Science / Engineering	Predictive Advertising	1: Someone's Always Watching You Online (Web article) 2: Video Games for Kids: Win or Lose? (essay)	*Key Skills* Reading for main ideas Making inferences *Additional Skills* Understanding key vocabulary Using your knowledge Scanning to predict content Reading for details Recognizing text type Synthesizing	Compound nouns Giving opinions	
4 WEATHER AND CLIMATE *Academic Disciplines* Environmental Studies / Meteorology	Tornadoes	1: Extreme Weather (profile) 2: Surviving the Sea of Sand: How to Stay Alive in the Sahara Desert (article)	*Key Skills* Reading for details Using your knowledge to predict content *Additional Skills* Understanding key vocabulary Reading for main ideas Recognizing text type Synthesizing	Collocations with *temperature* Describing a graph	

CRITICAL THINKING	GRAMMAR FOR WRITING	WRITING	ON CAMPUS
Using a T-chart Analyzing positives and negatives	Simple sentences 1: • Subject + verb *There is / there are*	*Academic Writing Skill* Capital letters and punctuation *Rhetorical Mode* Descriptive *Writing Task* Describe the place where you live. Write about its positives and its negatives. (sentences)	*Life Skill* Finding a place to live
Using an idea map to organize ideas	Simple sentences 2: • Objects and extra information • Prepositional phrases	*Academic Writing Skill* Organizing sentences into a paragraph *Rhetorical Mode* Descriptive *Writing Task* Describe a festival or special event. (paragraph)	*Life Skill* Cultural exchange
Analyzing a question	Connecting ideas • *And, also,* and *too* • Compound sentences • *However*	*Academic Writing Skill* Topic sentences *Rhetorical Mode* Opinion *Writing Task* The Internet wastes our time. It does not help us do more work. Do you agree or disagree? (paragraph)	*Study Skill* The virtual classroom
Analyzing a graph	Comparative and superlative adjectives	*Academic Writing Skills* Supporting sentences Giving examples • *Like, such as,* and *for example* *Rhetorical Mode* Descriptive *Writing Task* Describe the weather in a country or region. (paragraph)	*Life Skill* Seeing a doctor

UNIT	WATCH AND LISTEN	READINGS	READING SKILLS	LANGUAGE DEVELOPMENT	
5 SPORTS AND COMPETITION *Academic Disciplines* Sports Management / Sports Science	Skiing in the French Alps	1: Five Unusual Sports (article) 2: Tough Guy: A Race to the Limit (article)	*Key Skill* Scanning to predict content *Additional Skills* Understanding key vocabulary Previewing Reading for main ideas Reading for details Recognizing text type Understanding discourse Working out meaning Synthesizing	Prepositions of movement	
6 BUSINESS *Academic Disciplines* Business / Marketing	Amazon's Fulfillment Center	1: Are You Ready for the World of Work? (survey) 2: The Story of Google (article)	*Key Skills* Working out meaning from context Annotating a text *Additional Skills* Understanding key vocabulary Scanning to predict content Reading for main ideas Reading for details Identifying audience Making inferences Synthesizing	Collocations with *business* Business vocabulary	
7 PEOPLE *Academic Disciplines* Psychology / Sociology	The 101-Year-Old Weather Volunteer	1: Incredible People: Ben Underwood (blog post) 2: Incredible People (blog posts)	*Key Skill* Making inferences *Additional Skills* Understanding key vocabulary Scanning to predict content Reading for main ideas Reading for details Working out meaning Identifying purpose Synthesizing	Noun phrases with *of* Adjectives to describe people	
8 THE UNIVERSE *Academic Disciplines* Astronomy / Engineering	Going to the International Space Station	1: The Rise of Commercial Space Travel (article) 2: Life on Other Planets (essay)	*Key Skill* Identifying the author's purpose *Additional Skills* Understanding key vocabulary Using your knowledge Scanning to predict content Reading for main ideas Reading for details Making inferences Distinguishing fact from opinion Synthesizing	Giving evidence and supporting an argument	

CRITICAL THINKING	GRAMMAR FOR WRITING	WRITING	ON CAMPUS
Analyzing a diagram	Subject and verb agreement	*Academic Writing Skills* Ordering events in a process Removing unrelated information *Rhetorical Mode* Process *Writing Task* Describe the Sydney Triathlon. (paragraph)	*Communication Skill* Virtual communication

Using a timeline to put past events in order	The simple present and the simple past
	Time clauses with *when* to describe past events
		Academic Writing Skill
		Adding details to main facts
		
		Rhetorical Mode
		Narrative
		
		Writing Task
		Write about the history
		  of a business.
		  (paragraph)
			Study Skill
			Creating checklists

Using a Venn diagram	Modals of necessity	*Academic Writing Skill*
		Concluding sentences
		
		Rhetorical Mode
		Explanatory
		
		Writing Task
		Who do you think is a good
		  role model? Write a paragraph
		  explaining the qualities that make
		  that person a good role model.
		  (paragraph)
			Communication Skill
			Expressing your opinion

Evaluating arguments	*That* clauses in complex sentences
	Infinitives of purpose
		Academic Writing Skill
		Essay organization
		
		Rhetorical Mode
		Opinion
		
		Writing Task
		Should governments spend more
		  money on space exploration?
		  Give reasons and examples
		  to support your opinion.
		  (essay)
			Research Skill
			Using the library

HOW *PRISM* WORKS

1 Video

Setting the context

Every unit begins with a video clip. Each video serves as a springboard for the unit and introduces the topic in an engaging way. The clips were carefully selected to pique students' interest and prepare them to explore the unit's topic in greater depth. As they work, students develop key skills in prediction, comprehension, and discussion.

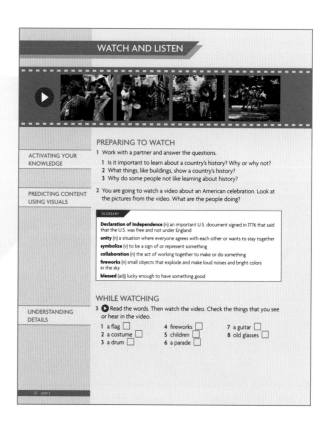

2 Reading

Receptive, language, and analytical skills

Students improve their reading abilities through a sequence of proven activities. They study key vocabulary to prepare them for each reading and to develop academic reading skills. A second reading leads into synthesis exercises that prepare students for college classrooms. Language Development sections teach vocabulary, collocations, and language structure.

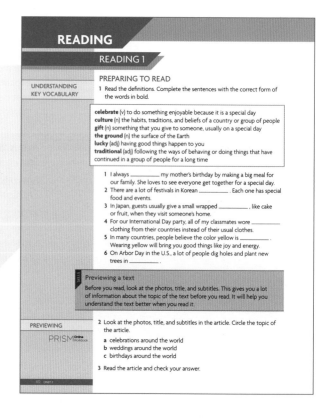

ACADEMIC WRITING SKILLS

ORGANIZING SENTENCES INTO A PARAGRAPH

In written English, sentences are organized into paragraphs. A paragraph is a group of sentences about the same topic. A new topic should be put in a new paragraph.

A paragraph has a *topic sentence*, *supporting sentences*, and a *concluding sentence*. A paragraph is often written in this order.
1 The **topic sentence** describes what the paragraph is about. It is usually the first sentence in a paragraph.
2 The **supporting sentences** tell more about the topic and give details and examples. They are in the middle of the paragraph.
3 The **concluding sentence** ends the paragraph. It usually summarizes the main idea in the paragraph. The concluding sentence often starts with phrases like *In conclusion*, *In summary*, or *In sum*. Some short paragraphs do not have a concluding sentence.

PRISM Online

1 Look at the sentences. They are from two different paragraphs. Paragraph 1 is about a city. Paragraph 2 is about a festival. Organize the sentences into two paragraphs. Write *1* or *2* next to each sentence.
a Popfest is a music festival in the U.K. __2__
b It is a very noisy city. __1__
c People wear waterproof shoes and coats. ____
d In the summer, it is very hot. ____
e It happens in July. ____
f I live in Taipei. ____
g There are lots of shops and restaurants. ____
h People listen to music and dance. ____
i It's a great place to live. ____

2 Read the paragraph and follow the steps.
1 Circle the topic sentence and write *T* next to it.
2 Underline the supporting sentences and write *S* next to them.
3 Highlight the concluding sentence and write *C* next to it.

> When I was a child, my favorite day of the year was my birthday. I always went to the park with my family. My sister and brother gave me presents, and we usually played games. We ate lunch, and then for dessert, we ate the chocolate cake my mother made. In sum, I have very special memories of my birthday.

52 UNIT 2

---

3 Writing

Critical thinking and production

Multiple critical thinking activities begin this section, preparing students for exercises that focus on grammar for writing and writing skills. All of these lead up to a structured writing task, in which students apply the skills and language they have developed over the course of the entire unit.

ON CAMPUS

THE VIRTUAL CLASSROOM

For many college classes, students have to do some work online. Professors expect students to be active both online and in class. Online participation is often part of a student's grade.

PREPARING TO READ
1 Work with a partner. Discuss the questions.
1 What do you do online for your classes?
2 How do you feel about online discussions? Why?
3 Do you prefer an online class or a face-to-face class? Why?
4 What are the advantages of online projects and discussions?

WHILE READING
2 Read part of a syllabus from a sociology class.

CLASS WEBSITE

For this class, students can find lecture notes and articles on the class website. Students will also use the class website to do the following tasks: submit[1] homework, take quizzes, do group projects, and post[2] responses for weekly discussions. Students should do the following:
• check the website each Monday for updates and assignments
• complete all tasks on time
• contact the professor by email if there is a problem

WEEKLY ONLINE DISCUSSIONS

Each Monday, a new question will be posted on the online discussion board. The discussion is open until Friday at 5 p.m. Students must actively participate in the discussion every week.

This part of the course counts for 25% of the final grade.
Students must do the following:
1 Post an answer to the question every week. Answers should be 30–40 words. Please post answer on Monday or Tuesday.
2 Respond to two classmates' answers. Responses should be 20–30 words.

All discussions should:
• be about the topic
• use complete sentences in paragraphs
• use academic language
• use correct spelling
• use good grammar
• be respectful of others

[1]**submit** (v) turn in, either online or to someone
[2]**post** (v) put on a website for others to see

78 UNIT 3

---

4 On Campus

Skills for college life

This unique section teaches students valuable skills beyond academic reading and writing. From asking questions in class to participating in a study group and from conducting research to finding help, students learn how to navigate university life. The section begins with a context-setting reading and moves directly into active practice of the skill.

WHAT MAKES *PRISM* SPECIAL: CRITICAL THINKING

Bloom's Taxonomy

In order to truly prepare for college coursework, students need to develop a full range of thinking skills. *Prism* teaches explicit critical thinking skills in every unit of every level. These skills adhere to the taxonomy developed by Benjamin Bloom. By working within the taxonomy, we are able to ensure that your students learn both lower-order and higher-order thinking skills.

Critical thinking exercises are accompanied by icons indicating where the activities fall in Bloom's Taxonomy.

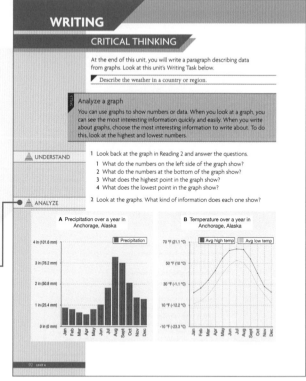

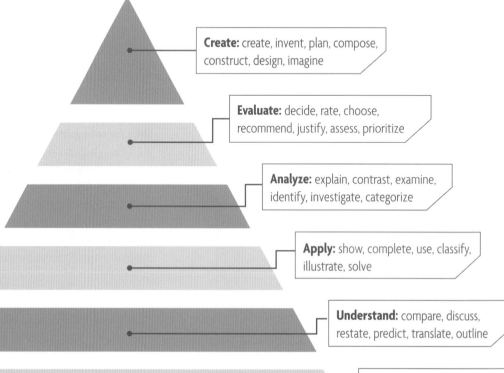

Create: create, invent, plan, compose, construct, design, imagine

Evaluate: decide, rate, choose, recommend, justify, assess, prioritize

Analyze: explain, contrast, examine, identify, investigate, categorize

Apply: show, complete, use, classify, illustrate, solve

Understand: compare, discuss, restate, predict, translate, outline

Remember: name, describe, relate, find, list, write, tell

WHAT MAKES *PRISM* SPECIAL: CRITICAL THINKING

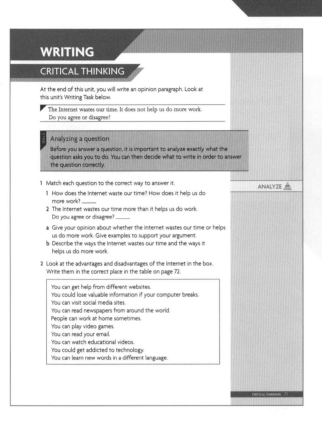

Create, **Evaluate**, and **Analyze** are critical skills for students in any college setting. Academic success depends on their abilities to derive knowledge from collected data, make educated judgments, and deliver insightful presentations. *Prism* helps students get there by creating activities such as categorizing information, comparing data, selecting the best solution to a problem, and developing arguments for a discussion or presentation.

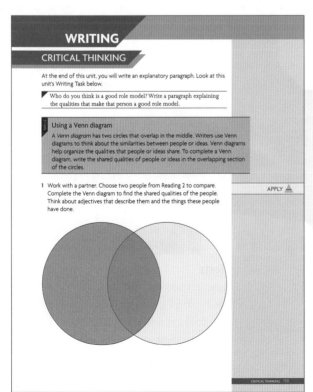

Apply, **Understand**, and **Remember** provide the foundation upon which all thinking occurs. Students need to be able to recall information, comprehend it, and see its use in new contexts. *Prism* develops these skills through exercises such as taking notes, mining notes for specific data, demonstrating comprehension, and distilling information from charts.

WHAT MAKES *PRISM* SPECIAL: ON CAMPUS

More college skills
Students need more than traditional academic skills. *Prism* teaches important skills for being engaged and successful all around campus, from emailing professors to navigating study groups.

Professors
Students learn how to take good lecture notes and how to communicate with professors and academic advisors.

Beyond the classroom
Skills include how to utilize campus resources, where to go for help, how to choose classes, and more.

Active learning
Students practice participating in class, in online discussion boards, and in study groups.

Texts
Learners become proficient at taking notes and annotating textbooks as well as conducting research online and in the library.

WHAT MAKES *PRISM* SPECIAL: RESEARCH

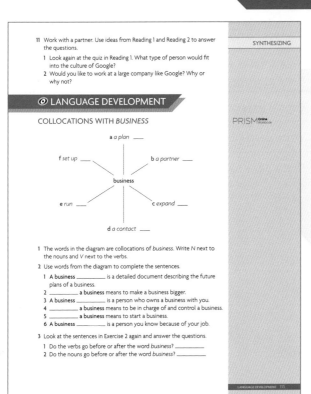

11 Work with a partner. Use ideas from Reading 1 and Reading 2 to answer the questions.

SYNTHESIZING

1 Look again at the quiz in Reading 1. What type of person would fit into the culture of Google?
2 Would you like to work at a large company like Google? Why or why not?

⊘ LANGUAGE DEVELOPMENT

COLLOCATIONS WITH *BUSINESS*

a *a plan* ____
f *set up* ____
b *a partner* ____
business
e *run* ____
c *expand* ____
d *a contact* ____

1 The words in the diagram are collocations of *business*. Write *N* next to the nouns and *V* next to the verbs.
2 Use words from the diagram to complete the sentences.
   1 A business _____ is a detailed document describing the future plans of a business.
   2 _____ a business means to make a business bigger.
   3 A business _____ is a person who owns a business with you.
   4 _____ a business means to be in charge of and control a business.
   5 _____ a business means to start a business.
   6 A business _____ is a person you know because of your job.
3 Look at the sentences in Exercise 2 again and answer the questions.
   1 Do the verbs go before or after the word *business*? _____
   2 Do the nouns go before or after the word *business*? _____

Vocabulary Research

Learning the right words

Students need to learn a wide range of general and academic vocabulary in order to be successful in college. *Prism* carefully selects the vocabulary that students study based on the General Service List, the Academic Word List, and the Cambridge English Corpus.

GRAMMAR FOR WRITING

SIMPLE SENTENCES 2

Objects and extra information

A simple sentence needs to have a *subject* and a *verb*. It must form a complete thought. The verb comes after the subject.
After the verb, there can be an *object* (usually a *noun* or *noun phrase*). You can also add extra information by using an *adjective* or a *prepositional phrase*.

subject	verb	noun phrase
I	visit	my family.

subject	verb	adjective
The people	are	happy.

subject	verb	prepositional phrase
The festival	is	in May.

1 Underline the subject and circle the verb in each sentence.
   1 The children wear traditional clothes.
   2 My family and I watch the fireworks.
   3 I visit my aunt and uncle.
   4 People in the U.S. celebrate college graduation.
   5 My parents and I go downtown.

2 Underline the words that come after the verb in each sentence. Then write *N* for noun, *A* for adjective, and *P* for prepositional phrase.
   1 My family eats at home. ____
   2 The costumes are beautiful. ____
   3 We exchange presents. ____
   4 I celebrate in the evening. ____
   5 The festival is traditional. ____

Grammar for Writing

Focused instruction

This unique feature teaches learners the exact grammar they will need for their writing task. With a focus on using grammar to accomplish rhetorical goals, these sections ensure that students learn the most useful grammar for their assignment.

LEARNING OBJECTIVES

Reading skill	Scan for numbers
Grammar	Nouns, verbs, and adjectives; simple sentences 1; *there is/there are*
Academic writing skill	Capital letters and punctuation
Writing Task	Write descriptive sentences
On Campus	Find a place to live

ACTIVATE YOUR KNOWLEDGE

Look at the photo and answer the questions.

1 Where is the place in the photo?

2 Is the city similar to or different from the place where you live? How?

3 Would you like to live here? Why or why not?

PREPARING TO WATCH

1 Work with a partner and answer the questions.

1 What makes a city beautiful?
2 Why might a city win an award?
3 Have you ever visited a beautiful city? If so, describe it.

2 You are going to watch a video about a city that won an award. Read the heading in the box and look at the pictures from the video. Then discuss the questions with your partner.

> "And the award for top U.S. city goes to ..."

1 What city do you think won the award?
2 Why do you think the city won the award?
3 What cities probably did not win the award?

GLOSSARY

beat out (phr v) to win something in a competition that someone else wants

Civil War (n) the war between the North (the Union) and the South (the Confederacy) in the United States from 1861 to 1865, which was won by the North

cuisine (n) a style of cooking

draw (n) something that people want to see or visit

regulate (v) to control an activity or process by rules or a system

tourism (n) the business of providing services for tourists

WHILE WATCHING

3 ▶ Read the sentences and then watch the video. Circle the correct answers.

1 Charleston is in *North / South* Carolina.
2 Charleston won against another city named *San Francisco / San Diego*.
3 This other city won the award for *13 / 18* years in a row.
4 People are *surprised / not surprised* when they come to Charleston.
5 There are a lot of *bus / horse carriage* rides in Charleston.
6 The tourism industry in Charleston is *not regulated / regulated*.
7 Tourism is a *small / big* business in Charleston.
8 More than three *million / billion* dollars are brought in by visitors a year.

4 ▶ Watch again and match the questions to the answers.

1 What is Charleston called?
2 Who is Joe Riley?
3 What can you feel all around Charleston?
4 What do people sell in the market?
5 What is one draw for visitors?
6 What things are regulated?

a buses and walking tours
b "the Holy City"
c the food
d the history
e the mayor
f handmade crafts

5 Work with a partner. Discuss the meanings of the underlined words from the video.

1 Charleston's many church <u>steeples</u> reach high into the sky.
2 Some of its houses were built two or three hundred years ago. They are two or three <u>centuries</u> old.
3 Tourists buy handmade crafts and souvenirs from <u>vendors</u> in the city market.
4 In Charleston, tourists often ride in horse <u>carriages</u> instead of cars.

DISCUSSION

6 Work in small groups. Discuss the questions.

1 Would you like to visit Charleston, South Carolina? Why or why not?
2 Think of one scene from the video and describe it to your group.
3 How is Charleston similar to your city or town? How is it different?

READING

PREPARING TO READ

1 You are going to read an article about cities. Read the sentences. Write the words in bold next to the definitions.

1 More than 8 million people live in New York City. New York City has the largest **population** in the United States.

2 The city hired an **expert** to help decide on the best place for the new shopping mall. He knows a lot about planning big cities.

3 People who live in big cities often visit the **countryside** so they can get away from the crowds and breathe some fresh air.

4 Studying in another country gives students the **opportunity** to learn about new cultures and see how other people live.

5 The sky was so gray with air **pollution** from cars and factory smoke that I couldn't see the sunset.

6 Shanghai is thousands of years old, but it is also a very **modern** city. It is filled with tall glass buildings and bright lights.

7 Big cities usually have a lot of **traffic**, especially when people drive to work in the morning and drive home in the evening.

8 Washington, D.C., is the **capital** of the United States. It is where the U.S. government is run.

a _____ (n) the cars, trucks, and other vehicles using a road

b _____ (n) land that is not in towns or cities and may have farms and fields

c _____ (adj) designed and made using the most recent ideas and methods

d _____ (n) the number of people living in a place

e _____ (n) damage caused to water, air, and land by harmful materials or waste

f _____ (n) the most important city in a country or state; where the government is

g _____ (n) someone who has a lot of skill in or a lot of knowledge about something

h _____ (n) a chance to do or experience something good

2 Read the title of the article. What do you think *mega* means?

a very busy   b very good   c very big

3 Read the article and check your answer.

Rise of the MEGACITIES

Megacity: A City with More Than Ten Million People

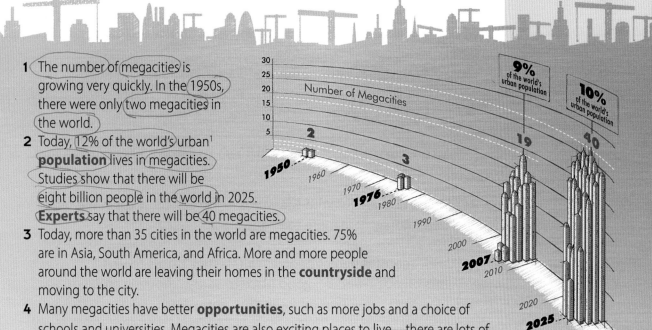

1 The number of megacities is growing very quickly. In the 1950s, there were only two megacities in the world.

2 Today, 12% of the world's urban[1] **population** lives in megacities. Studies show that there will be eight billion people in the world in 2025. **Experts** say that there will be 40 megacities.

3 Today, more than 35 cities in the world are megacities. 75% are in Asia, South America, and Africa. More and more people around the world are leaving their homes in the **countryside** and moving to the city.

4 Many megacities have better **opportunities**, such as more jobs and a choice of schools and universities. Megacities are also exciting places to live—there are lots of different people, languages, and restaurants, and there are many interesting things to do.

5 However, megacities have problems, too. The cities are very big, and this can cause problems like **pollution** or poor housing[2].

Chart labels: Number of Megacities; 30, 25, 20, 15, 10, 5; 1950 — 2; 1976 — 3; 2007 — 19 (9% of the world's urban population); 2025 — 40 (10% of the world's urban population); 1960, 1970, 1980, 1990, 2000, 2010, 2020, 2030

TOKYO, JAPAN
37.8 MILLION

6 Tokyo is an exciting **modern** city in the east of Japan. There are lots of jobs because most big companies in Japan are in Tokyo. It is also an excellent place to study—20% of Japan's universities are in the city. However, Tokyo is very busy, and the **traffic** is very bad. More than 8.7 million people use the subway every day.

DELHI, INDIA
25 MILLION

7 Delhi is in the north of India. It has many beautiful monuments[3], interesting museums, and modern restaurants. There is an exciting mix of different cultures in the city, and there are four official languages: Hindi, Urdu, Punjabi, and English. However, there are not enough houses in some parts of Delhi. This means that many people live in large slums in the city.

CAIRO, EGYPT
16.9 MILLION

8 Cairo is the **capital** of Egypt, and it is the largest city in Africa. Cairo has important car and film industries. The city is the center of many government offices and has many universities, one of which is over 1,200 years old.

[1]**urban** (adj) relating to towns and cities
[2]**housing** (n) places to live, such as apartments or houses
[3]**monuments** (n) old buildings or places that are important in history

WHILE READING

4 Write *T* (true) or *F* (false) next to the statements. Then correct the false sentences.

_____ 1 There are more megacities now than in 1950.

_____

_____ 2 There are many opportunities to study in megacities.

_____

_____ 3 Many people leave the countryside and move to a city.

_____

_____ 4 Almost 35 cities in the world are megacities.

_____

_____ 5 Most megacities are in Europe.

_____

_____ 6 Finding a house or an apartment to live in is easy in megacities.

_____

5 Read the article again. Write the words in the correct place in the table. Some words may fit in more than one place.

> mix of different people   interesting places to visit
> lots of jobs   traffic   good place to study   housing problem
> important industries   busy trains

Tokyo	
Delhi	
Cairo	

Scanning for numbers

When scanning a text, readers look for specific information and details. Do not read the whole text. Readers often scan a text to find important numbers, percentages, and dates.

6 Find and circle all the numbers in the article.

7 Complete the student's notes with the correct numbers from the article.

SCANNING TO FIND INFORMATION

PRISM Online Workbook

1 number of megacities in 1950 = _____
2 predicted number of megacities in 2025 = _____
3 percent of urban population in the world that live in megacities = _____ %
4 expected global population in 2025 = _____ billion
5 number of people who use the subway in Tokyo = _____ million
6 percent of Japanese universities in Tokyo = _____ %
7 number of people living in Delhi = _____ million
8 number of official languages spoken in Delhi = _____
9 age of Cairo's oldest university = over _____ years old

READING BETWEEN THE LINES

8 Look at the word *slums* underlined in the article. What do you think it means? Circle the correct answer.

a a very poor and crowded area in a city
b a very unclean house
c a very expensive area in the center of a city

WORKING OUT MEANING

DISCUSSION

9 Work with a partner. Discuss the questions.

1 Are there any megacities in or near your country?
2 What are the advantages and disadvantages of living in the city?
3 Why are modern cities growing so quickly?
4 What are the best solutions to the problems of pollution and poor housing?

READING 2

PREPARING TO READ

PRISM Online Workbook

1 Read the definitions. Complete the sentences with the correct form of the words in bold.

> **area** (n) a region or part of a larger place, like a country or city
> **cheap** (adj) not expensive, or costs less than usual
> **downtown** (adj) the main or central part of a city
> **expensive** (adj) costs a lot of money; not cheap
> **local** (adj) relating to a particular area, city, or town
> **noisy** (adj) loud; makes a lot of noise
> **quiet** (adj) makes little or no noise

1 My hotel is ___quiet___ and calm. It is outside of the busy city center, so it isn't loud at night.
2 Central Park is a nice ___area___ to relax in New York City.
3 When people visit new cities, it's a good idea to ask ___local___ people for the best restaurants. They know the most about their city.
4 Since the airline was new, they offered ___cheap___ flights from New York City to Boston. A lot of new customers bought tickets at low prices.
5 We took the bus to ___downtown___ Chicago because that is where the main tourist sites in the city are located.
6 It's getting more ___expensive___ to live in a big city, so people who can't pay the high prices are moving away.
7 There was a lot of traffic on my street last night. There were so many ___noisy___, loud cars that I couldn't sleep.

2 Read the title of the article on page 23. What general topic do you think the article is about?

a geography
b tourism
c history

3 Read the introduction and check your answer.

4 Circle the word or words in the introduction that tell you the answer.

HOMESTAY VACATIONS
A Home away from Home

1   Homestays are becoming more and more popular, and people around the world are offering their homes as hotels. Homestays offer **cheap** places to stay and the chance for guests to see the **area** like **local** people. They are very popular with students who want to stay in another country and learn a language. We asked three families who run homestays to tell us about where they live.

a _____

The Atal family

2   Our family home is in the north of Nepal, in the Himalayan Mountains, in the village[1] of Manang. The village is small and very **quiet**. It is a very friendly place. The mountains are extremely beautiful. You can go for long walks and swim in the rivers, but there are no stores, movie theaters, or cafés.

b _____

Kate and Julian Foxton

3   Our two-bedroom house is in Washington State, in the U.S. It is in the Pacific Northwest. It is a 20-minute drive to the nearest city, Seattle. There are a lot of lakes, rivers, and forests, and it is very quiet. We spend a lot of time reading books, watching movies, and going for walks in the forest, where we see a lot of flowers and small animals. Our area is great for sports like hiking, kayaking, and mountain biking. However, the houses here are **expensive**, which can be a problem for local people. There aren't many buses or trains here, so it can be difficult to get around without a car.

c _____

Chafic and Aline Halwany

4   Our home is near the historic **downtown** area of Beirut, Lebanon, one of the largest cities in the Middle East. There are lots of cafés and restaurants, which are open late at night. We love it here because it's so friendly and you can always find what you need—lots of people come to learn Arabic and French. There are also a lot of jobs and businesses here. However, it can be **noisy** at night, and there is a lot of traffic during the day. The best thing about Beirut is the weather. It is nice all year round; it rains in the winter, but there is no snow.

[1]**village** (n) a very small town in the countryside

WHILE READING

5 Write the headings above the matching paragraphs in the article.

A Big City
A Mountain Village
A House near the Forest

6 Look at the summaries of the paragraphs. Cross out the incorrect words in bold and write the correct words. The first one has been done for you as an example.

1 The Atal family lives in a ~~city~~ *village*. It is a **busy** place. The mountains are

very **cold**.

2 Kate and Julian Foxton live in the **Northeast** *Washington* of the United States.

The area is great for **theaters**. The houses are really **cheap**.

3 Chafic and Aline Halwany live in a **small** city. People learn **English** and

French in the downtown area. There is a lot of traffic **at night**.

READING BETWEEN THE LINES

7 Work with a partner. Discuss the questions.

1 Why are homestays cheap places to stay?
2 How many languages do the Halwanys speak?
3 Do Kate and Julian have children?

DISCUSSION

8 Work with a partner. Discuss the questions.

1 Why do people go to villages or to the countryside on vacation?
2 What are the advantages and disadvantages of living in the countryside?
3 Why do young people leave the countryside to live in the city?
4 Use information from Reading 1 and Reading 2 to answer the questions. Think of a large city that you know. What do local people do for fun? What do people who visit the city on vacation do for fun? Do you think local people and tourists do the same things?

NOUNS, VERBS, AND ADJECTIVES

LANGUAGE

A *noun* refers to a person, place, or thing. *girl*
A *verb* describes an action. *run*
An *adjective* describes a noun. *tall*

| noun | verb | | adjective | adjective | noun | | noun | |
| **Jenny** | **swam** | in the | **warm** | **blue** | **sea** | on her | **vacation** | last year. |

1   Look at the sentence and the numbered words. Match the numbers to
    the parts of speech.

PRISM | Online Workbook

> (1) Delhi (2) has many (3) beautiful (1) monuments,
> (3) interesting (1) museums and (3) modern (1) restaurants.
>
> noun   1_____
> verb   2_____
> adjective   3_____

2   Write the words from the box in the correct places in the table.

> live   town   excellent   drive   exciting
>   have   café   different   building

noun	verb	adjective
Town	live	excellent
café	drive	exciting
building	have	different

Adjectives

Adjectives describe nouns. Use the structure *adjective + noun*.

	adjective	*+ noun*
Beirut is an	**interesting**	**city**.
There are many	**excellent**	**restaurants**.

Adjectives are never plural.

a different place → ~~some differents places~~ → some different places

3 Match the adjectives to their opposites.

1 interesting   **a** expensive
2 cheap   **b** boring
3 polluted   **c** clean
4 beautiful   **d** quiet
5 noisy   **e** ugly

4 Complete the sentences with adjectives from Exercise 3.

1 There are lots of cars and traffic jams. The air is very _polluted_ .
2 This is a(n) _expensive_ city. Everything costs a lot of money.
3 My town is very _quiet_ . There isn't any noise.
4 Chicago is a really _interesting_ place. There are lots of things to do.
5 The building looks horrible. It's very _ugly_ .

a traffic jam

WRITING

CRITICAL THINKING

At the end of this unit, you will write six descriptive sentences. Look at this unit's Writing Task below.

> Describe the place where you live. Write about its positives and its negatives.

1 What are the main differences between the places described in Reading 1 and the places in Reading 2?

UNDERSTAND ▲

2 Read the notes about living in a city from Reading 2. Which notes are positive and which notes are negative? Write + or −.

ANALYZE ▲

1 lots of cafés and restaurants __+__
2 places stay open late at night __+__
3 a lot of traffic __−__
4 a lot of people __−__
5 it can be noisy __−__
6 a lot of jobs and businesses __+__

SKILLS

Using a T-chart

You can use a T-chart to write about positives (+) and negatives (−). Write about the positives in one column and the negatives in the other column.

---

3 Write the notes from Exercise 2 in the correct place in the T-chart.

positive (+)	negative (−)
lots of cafés and restaurants places stay open late at night a lot of jobs and businesses nature	a lot of traffic a lot of people It can be noise Polution

4 Think of two more positives and two more negatives about living in a city. Write them in the T-chart in Exercise 3.

5 Think of positives and negatives about living in a small town. Write information from Reading 2 and your own ideas in the T-chart.

positive (+)	negative (–)
beautiful	not many buses or trains

CREATE

6 Think about where you live or where you are from. What are the positives and negatives about this place? Think about the things in the list and create a T-chart like the one in Exercise 5.

- things to do
- jobs
- transportation
- people
- houses

GRAMMAR FOR WRITING

SIMPLE SENTENCES 1

LANGUAGE

Subject + verb

A *simple sentence* is a complete thought that includes a subject and a verb. The subject of a sentence can be a noun or a noun phrase. A noun phrase is a group of words that acts like a noun. The verb can also be one word or a group of words.

subject (noun or noun phrase)	verb	
The people in the town	are	friendly.
The village	does not have	a shop.
My brother	lives	in the city.

Remember that a sentence is a *complete* thought.
✔ My brother lives in the city. (complete sentence)
✘ lives in the city. (missing a subject)
✘ My brother in the city. (missing a verb)

1 Underline the subject and circle the verb in the sentences.

    1 Paris is a beautiful city.
    2 The town does not have a park.
    3 I live in a small town.
    4 Istanbul has many attractions.
    5 Many students live in the city.
    6 The village is not very exciting.
    7 The stores are excellent.
    8 The houses in the town are not very expensive.

2 Write simple sentences with the words. Write *S* next to the subject and *V* next to the verb in each sentence.

    1 I / Mexican _____ .
    2 He / an engineer _____ .
    3 The people / nice _____ .
    4 We / happy _____ .
    5 Seattle / beautiful _____ .
    6 It / a small town _____ .

THERE IS / THERE ARE

LANGUAGE

Use *there is (not) / there are (not)* to explain the general features of a place. These sentences do not use a subject.

There is a small beach with white sand.
There are many local cafés.

Contractions: *there's*, *there isn't*, *there aren't*

Use *there is (not)* to talk about one thing (singular) and *there are (not)* to talk about many things (plural).

	there is (not) / there are (not)	noun / noun phrase
singular	There is	a lake.
	There isn't	a movie theater.
plural	There are	a lot of shops.
	There aren't	many beaches.

3 Circle the correct words to complete the sentences.

1 There *isn't / aren't* many traffic jams in my town.
2 There *is / are* an excellent museum.
3 There *isn't / aren't* people from many different countries.
4 There *is / are* lots of apartments in the downtown area.
5 There *is / are* a beach.
6 There *isn't / aren't* many jobs.

4 Rewrite the sentences with the correct form of *there is (not) / there are (not)*.

1 Many restaurants are not in my town.
   <u>There aren't many restaurants in my town.</u>

2 A famous museum is in my city.
   _____

3 A lake is not in my town.
   _____

4 A lot of cars are in my city.
   _____

5 Many expensive stores are in my city.
   _____

6 A quiet park is in my town.
   _____

7 Many people are not in my town.
   _____

5 Read the fact file about the city of Doha in Qatar. Then write one sentence for each item using *there is (not) / there are (not)*.

FACT FILE DOHA, QATAR

- many sports stadiums
- lots of museums
- twelve universities
- a port
- one airport
- many five-star hotels
- a castle
- no subway system

1 There are many sports stadiums.
2 _____
3 _____
4 _____
5 _____
6 _____
7 _____
8 _____

ACADEMIC WRITING SKILLS

CAPITAL LETTERS AND PUNCTUATION

Use a *capital letter* at the beginning of a sentence. Use a *period* (.) at the end of a sentence.
He lives in Abu Dhabi.

Use *commas* (,) to separate three or more items in a list.
In her free time, she likes **to read, exercise, and play video games**.

Use a capital letter with a *proper noun* (the name of a specific person, place, or thing).

| France | Istanbul | July | Saturday |

Always use a capital letter for *I*.   I live in London.

1 Work with a partner. Correct the punctuation and capital letters in the paragraph.

PRISM Online Workbook

> I
> i live in montreal it is a city in canada it is a beautiful city there
> are many stores and restaurants the people are friendly there is an art
> festival in june people in montreal speak both french and english it is
> very crowded with tourists in the summer in the winter, people like
> to ice skate and cross-country ski

Describe the place where you live. Write about its positives and its negatives.

PLAN

1 Look at the T-chart you made in Critical Thinking. Choose three positives and three negatives that you are going to write about.

2 Refer to the Task Checklist on page 33 as you prepare your sentences.

WRITE A FIRST DRAFT

3 Write three sentences describing positive things and three sentences describing negative things about where you live.

positive 1	
positive 2	
positive 3	
negative 1	
negative 2	
negative 3	

REVISE

4 Use the Task Checklist to review your sentences for content and structure.

TASK CHECKLIST	✔
Did you write about the place where you live?	
Did you write six sentences?	
Are there three positive sentences?	
Are there three negative sentences?	

5 Make any necessary changes to your sentences.

EDIT

6 Use the Language Checklist to edit your sentences for language errors.

LANGUAGE CHECKLIST	✔
Did you use nouns, verbs, and adjectives correctly?	
Does every sentence have a subject and a verb?	
Did you use the correct form of *there is / there are*?	
Did you use capital letters, commas, and periods correctly?	

7 Make any necessary changes to your sentences.

ON CAMPUS

FINDING A PLACE TO LIVE

It's important to find the right place to live because it makes the college experience better. Most college campuses have information about housing, both on and off campus.

PREPARING TO READ

1 Work with a partner. Discuss the questions.

1 Describe the place where you live and the people you live with.

2 What is important to you when choosing a place to live?

☐ close to campus ☐ near the bus ☐ quiet neighborhood
☐ living with others ☐ living alone ☐ furnished
☐ living with native ☐ laundry ☐ parking space
English speakers

3 Where do you get information about housing near your school?

WHILE READING

2 Read four listings for available rentals on the website for the housing office on page 35. Write descriptions in the correct column in the table.

| pay a deposit share a room take a bus share a bathroom |
| live alone includes meals includes activities on campus |
| free parking unfurnished pay for parking near campus |

shared house	dorm	apartment	homestay

Listings

 Furnished room available in 7-bedroom shared house

Shared bathroom and kitchen
One block from campus
Parking space (free)
No pets, no smokers
$650/month + utilities[1]

 Unfurnished 1-bedroom apartment

Near campus. Free Wi-Fi and cable.
Parking available ($50/month).
Laundry room in building.
$950/month. $500 security deposit.
Utilities included.

Do you want more information about campus housing?
Come to the Campus Dorm Open House, McCarty Hall, May 3, 10:00 a.m. till noon.
Come learn more about our:

- Helpful RAs[2]
- Nice double rooms
- Great meal plans
- Fun activities
- Bike storage

It's easy to meet people. And the dorm is right on campus!

Homestay near campus

We are a family with 2 small children. We would like to welcome an international student to join our family. It's a great chance to speak English!
We have a quiet, sunny room with bathroom available for $525/month. Includes two meals a day, free laundry, and free parking. Our home is 20 minutes from campus on the #70 bus.
Email Northwest Homestays for an appointment.

[1] **utilities** (n) electricity, gas, water
[2] **RA** (n) resident assistant; a trained student leader in a dorm

PRACTICE

3 Imagine you are looking for a new place to live. Look at the four listings on the website. Write one positive sentence and one negative sentence about each one. Which place do you prefer? Why?

REAL-WORLD APPLICATION

4 Work with a partner. Visit the housing office at your school or the housing office website.

1 Find three listings for student housing.
2 Make a list of the positive and negative things about each listing. Choose your favorite.
3 Report back to your class. Describe the positive and negative things about your favorite listing. Explain why you prefer it.

LEARNING OBJECTIVES

Reading skill	Preview a text
Grammar	Prepositions of time and place; adverbs of frequency; simple sentences 2
Academic writing skill	Organize sentences into a paragraph
Writing Task	Write a descriptive paragraph
On Campus	Cultural exchange

FESTIVALS AND CELEBRATIONS

ACTIVATE YOUR KNOWLEDGE

Work with a partner. Look at the photos and discuss the questions.

1 Where is the place in the large photo? What is happening in the photo?

2 What is happening in the small photos?

3 What countries do you think the photos are from?

PREPARING TO WATCH

ACTIVATING YOUR KNOWLEDGE

1 Work with a partner and answer the questions.

1 Is it important to learn about a country's history? Why or why not?
2 What things, like buildings, show a country's history?
3 Why do some people not like learning about history?

PREDICTING CONTENT USING VISUALS

2 You are going to watch a video about an American celebration. Look at the pictures from the video. What are the people doing?

fife = flauta

> **GLOSSARY**
>
> **Declaration of Independence** (n) an important U.S. document signed in 1776 that said that the U.S. was free and not under England
>
> **unity** (n) a situation where everyone agrees with each other or wants to stay together
>
> **symbolize** (v) to be a sign of or represent something
>
> **collaboration** (n) the act of working together to make or do something
>
> **fireworks** (n) small objects that explode and make loud noises and bright colors in the sky
>
> **blessed** (adj) lucky enough to have something good

WHILE WATCHING

UNDERSTANDING DETAILS

3 ▶ Read the words. Then watch the video. Check the things that you see or hear in the video.

1 a flag ☐   4 fireworks ☐   7 a guitar ☐
2 a costume ☐   5 children ☐   8 old glasses ☐
3 a drum ☐   6 a parade ☐

Kick off = beginning start something

, Watch the Great Gats by F. Scott Fitzgerald

4 ▶ Watch again. Choose the correct answers.

1 The young Americans are talking about __b__ .
   a Flag Day   **b** Independence Day
2 The holiday is on __a__ .
   a July 4   **b** June 4
3 This celebration is in __b__ .
   a Washington, D.C.   **b** Philadelphia
4 The people are celebrating the date the United States __a__ .
   a became independent   **b** won a war
5 What do many children like about this day?
   a the fireworks   **b** the costumes

5 Match the sentence halves to form the ideas of the speakers in the video.

1 It symbolizes   4 **a** to be American.
2 The fireworks   3 **b** to celebrate every year.
3 It's a great day   5 **c** to live in this country.
4 We are blessed   1 **d** the unity of the country.
5 It's an important day for Americans 2 **e** are really fun.

UNDERSTANDING
MAIN IDEAS

6 Why is celebrating this day important for young Americans?
   Choose the best answer.

   a They think about their history.
   b They learn about fireworks.
   c They have a fun time.

MAKING INFERENCES

DISCUSSION

7 Work in small groups. Discuss the questions.

1 What are some interesting ways to learn about history?
2 What are some important dates in your country's history?
3 How do people celebrate these days?

distinctive architecture.

READING

READING 1

PREPARING TO READ

1 Read the definitions. Complete the sentences with the correct form of the words in bold.

> **celebrate** (v) to do something enjoyable because it is a special day
> **culture** (n) the habits, traditions, and beliefs of a country or group of people
> **gift** (n) something that you give to someone, usually on a special day
> **the ground** (n) the surface of the Earth
> **lucky** (adj) having good things happen to you
> **traditional** (adj) following the ways of behaving or doing things that have continued in a group of people for a long time

1 I always ___celebrate___ my mother's birthday by making a big meal for our family. She loves to see everyone get together for a special day.
2 There are a lot of festivals in Korean ___tradition___ . Each one has special food and events.
3 In Japan, guests usually give a small wrapped ___gift___ , like cake or fruit, when they visit someone's home.
4 For our International Day party, all of my classmates wore ___culture___ clothing from their countries instead of their usual clothes.
5 In many countries, people believe the color yellow is ___lucky___ . Wearing yellow will bring you good things like joy and energy.
6 On Arbor Day in the U.S., a lot of people dig holes and plant new trees in ___the ground___ .

SKILLS

Previewing a text

Before you read, look at the photos, title, and subtitles. This gives you a lot of information about the topic of the text before you read. It will help you understand the text better when you read it.

2 Look at the photos, title, and subtitles in the article. Circle the topic of the article.

a celebrations around the world
b weddings around the world
c birthdays around the world

3 Read the article and check your answer.

PRISM Online Workbook

Celebrate!

Piñatas

1   In Mexico, children often have piñatas on their birthday. The child's parents put chocolates and other candy inside the piñata and hang it on a tree. Then the children hit the piñata with a stick. It breaks, and the candy falls out onto the ground.

Noodles

2   In China, people **celebrate** weddings with an eight-course meal because the word *eight* sounds like the word for *good luck*. The last dish of the meal is always noodles. The noodles are long and thin. You have to eat them in one piece—you can't cut them. In Chinese **culture**, long noodles are **lucky**. Long noodles mean you will have a long life.

Mother's Day

3   Many people around the world honor their mothers on Mother's Day. In the U.S., Mother's Day is always celebrated on the second Sunday in May. Sons and daughters like to give their mother a day to rest, so they might surprise her by cleaning the house or cooking a nice meal for her. They also give her **gifts** such as flowers or jewelry. Many families take their mother to a restaurant for lunch or dinner.

Name Days

4   As well as a birthday, many people in southern Europe also celebrate their name day. In Greece, name days are more important than birthdays. People have big parties and open their houses to anybody who wants to come. People bring small gifts, often flowers or a box of candy.

Coming of Age Day

5   In Japan, people celebrate Coming of Age Day, or *Seijin no hi*, on the second Monday in January. On this holiday, Japan congratulates people who have turned 20 years old between April 2 of the last year to April 1 of the current year. In Japanese culture, this is the age when teenagers become adults and take on the responsibilities of being an adult. Young women usually wear a **traditional** *furisode* kimono, while young men often wear Western style suits, and they attend a ceremony[1] in their area. They receive small gifts and celebrate with their friends after the ceremony.

[1]**ceremony** (n) a formal event that people go to, often for a holiday or to celebrate someone or something

WHILE READING

4 Read the article again. Write the name of the country next to the description of the celebration.

1 use a stick to get candy ___pinata___
2 eat long noodles ___Noodle___
3 celebrate a day more important than a birthday ___name day___
4 wear traditional clothes _____
5 second Sunday in May ___mother day___

5 Read the article again and write *T* (true) or *F* (false) next to the statements. Then correct the false statements.

_F_ 1 Piñatas have flowers inside them.

_____

_F_ 2 Long noodles are unlucky in Chinese culture.

_____

_F_ 3 Mother's Day in the U.S. is the first week in May.

_____

_T_ 4 On name days, people bring gifts.

_____

_T_ 5 On Coming of Age Day, people wear special clothes.

_____

READING BETWEEN THE LINES

6 Where would you find this article? Circle the correct answer.

a in a magazine
b in an academic journal

7 Circle the features that helped you find the answer.

> photos   color of text   length of paragraphs   title
> number of paragraphs   design of the article

DISCUSSION

8 Work with a partner. Discuss the questions.

1 What birthdays and special days do you celebrate?
2 What do you do on these days?
3 What is your favorite celebration? Why?

PREPARING TO READ

UNDERSTANDING
KEY VOCABULARY

PRISM Online Workbook

1 You are going to read about the Muscat Festival in Oman. Before you read, circle the best definition for the words or phrases in bold.

1 The children enjoyed a lot of **activities** at the birthday party. They had their faces painted, played games, and pet different animals.
   a things people do for fun
   b things people say

2 The end of the Civil War is an important day in U.S. **history**.
   a events that are happening now
   b the whole series of events in the past that relate to the development of a country, subject, or person

3 Carnival in Rio de Janeiro, Brazil, is a very **popular** event. Millions of people watch the parades for several days.
   a liked by many people
   b disliked by many people

4 The **highlight** of every holiday is getting together with loved ones.
   a location
   b most enjoyable part

5 Nearly everyone in town **takes part in** the race. There is a shorter race for children and a longer one for adults.
   a does an activity with other people
   b eats special types of food

6 Thousands of **visitors** went to the museum on the first day it opened.
   a people who organize a party and invite guests
   b people who go to see a person or a place

> **SKILLS**
>
> *Proper nouns* are names of people, countries, cities, festivals, and nationalities. Days of the week and months are also proper nouns.

2 Read paragraph 1 in the text on page 44 and circle the proper nouns.

SCANNING TO
PREDICT CONTENT

Carnival in Rio de Janeiro, Brazil

WHILE READING

3 Read the text. Write the paragraph number next to the ideas. Underline the information in the text that helped you find the answer.

a the countries people visit from   Paragraph _____

b how long the Muscat Festival lasts   Paragraph _____

c different events in the festival   Paragraph _____

d international culture   Paragraph _____

e the Tour of Oman   Paragraph _____

Muscat Festival

1 One of the most important festivals in Oman is the Muscat Festival. The festival lasts for about one month and takes place in February every year. During the festival, many **activities** are available for people to **take part in**.

2 Large numbers of people, including local Omanis and **visitors** to Oman, go to the different events. The events are a celebration of both Omani and international **history** and traditions. The events take place in different places across the country. Many businesses show their products for people to look at and buy.

3 The Muscat Festival also includes the very **popular** six-day Tour of Oman bike race. Professional cyclists from around the world take part in the race. The race is 620 miles (1,000 kilometers) long, and it takes the cyclists up the beautiful Jabal Al Akhdhar—the Green Mountain.

4 Other **highlights** of the Muscat Festival include the chance to try out different types of food at the Oman Food Festival. The Muscat Art Festival also offers Arabic music, concerts and plays, and other entertainment for the whole family. The Festival of Lights is one of the most popular events at the Muscat Festival.

5 The Muscat Festival is an international event, with people visiting from countries as far away as Brazil and Cuba. Visitors also arrive from Italy, India, Russia, South Korea, Spain, Tunisia, and Turkey, as well as many other countries. They enjoy the amazing clothes, food, and music. Some people just enjoy the mix of different cultures.

participate

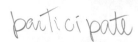

4 Read the text again. Complete the sentences with information from the text.

   1 The Muscat Festival happens in the month of _____ .

   2 People from all over the world _____ the festival.

   3 The English name for the Jabal Al Akhdhar is the _____ .

   4 You can see plays at the _____ .

   5 The Festival of Lights is a very _____ event.

   6 Visitors enjoy clothes, _____ , and _____ .

READING BETWEEN THE LINES

5 Where would you find this text?

   a in a textbook on the culture of Oman

   b in a textbook on the economy of Oman

6 What other topics would you expect to find in the book? Add two more topics to the list.

   1 _food_   3 _____

   2 _theater_   4 _____

DISCUSSION

7 Work with a partner. Discuss the questions.

   1 Would you like to visit Oman?

   2 What information about festivals in your country would you give a visitor? Answer the questions.

      a What is the festival?

      b When is it?

      c Where is it?

      d What happens?

   3 Use information from Reading 1 and Reading 2 to compare the celebrations you read about with other celebrations you know. How are they the same? How are they different?

   4 In what ways do festivals teach you about culture?

PREPOSITIONS OF TIME AND PLACE

LANGUAGE

Use *on* with a specific date or day and with *the weekend / weekends*.
My birthday is **on** May 1 / **on** Saturday.
I like to sleep late **on** weekends.

Use *in* with a month and with *the morning, the afternoon,* and *the evening.*
Use *in* with a country, city, or town.
My birthday is **in** May.
We eat breakfast **in** the morning.
We have an apartment **in** France / **in** Paris.

Use *at* with a specific time and with *night.*
Use *at* with *school, work,* and *home.*
We eat dinner **at** seven o'clock **at** night.
We have a party **at** school.

PRISM Online Workbook

1 Write the words from the box in the correct place in the table.

> school   June   Sunday   home   work   a town
> Istanbul   the evening   the morning   night   January 1
> my country   Brazil   eight o'clock   Tuesday

	on	*in*	*at*
places			
times			

2 Complete the sentences with *on, in,* or *at.*

1 People have parties _____ work with their colleagues.
2 We have a big family meal _____ Saturday.
3 The festival is _____ November.
4 My brother's wedding is _____ December 2.
5 The children wake up _____ seven o'clock.
6 People celebrate Thanksgiving _____ the U.S.
7 We stay _____ home for the whole weekend.
8 We eat dinner late _____ night.
9 We meet our friends _____ the weekend.

ADVERBS OF FREQUENCY

Use adverbs of frequency to talk about habits. They describe how often someone does something. Adverbs of frequency usually go before the verb in a sentence.

In Mexico, children **often** have piñatas on their birthday.
In China, my family **always** celebrates weddings with
an eight-course meal.
Children in the U.S. **sometimes** clean the house on Mother's Day.
During Eid, people **usually** visit family and friends.
My family **never** cuts their noodles at a wedding in China.

0%				100%
never	sometimes	often	usually	always

3 Complete the sentences with adverbs of frequency. Write sentences that are true for you.

1 I _____ visit my parents on the holidays.
2 I _____ give my friends a present on their birthday.
3 I _____ celebrate New Year's Eve.
4 I _____ go to weddings.
5 I _____ eat candy on special occasions.

4 Work with a partner. Compare and discuss your answers.

5 Put the words in order to make complete sentences.

1 in the evening / usually starts / The music / eight o'clock / at / .

_____

2 cake / my birthday / on / always eat / I / .

_____

3 to call / She / forgets / never / her family / .

_____

4 sometimes get / toys / money instead of / The children / .

_____

5 it / in February / In New York, / often snows / .

_____

WRITING

CRITICAL THINKING

At the end of this unit, you will write a descriptive paragraph. Look at this unit's Writing Task below.

▶ Describe a festival or special event.

Using an idea map to organize ideas

Before you write, you need to decide what to write about. An idea map can help you organize your ideas.

 APPLY

1 Complete the idea map with information from Reading 2.

   1 Write the name of the event in the center of the idea map.

   2 Write about the topics in the correct part of the idea map.

- when the event is
- where the event is
- what people eat and drink at the event
- what people do at the event
- what people wear to the event

FOOD & DRINKS:

_____

_____

_____

WHERE: ACTIVITIES:

_____   _____

_____   _____

_____   _____

NAME:

_____

WHEN: CLOTHES:

_____   _____

_____   _____

_____   _____

2 Compare your idea map with a partner. Did you include the same information?

3 Work with a partner. Think about any festivals or celebrations that you both know about. Discuss them with your partner and choose one to write about.

4 Complete the idea map with information about the festival or celebration you chose in Exercise 3. You will use this to brainstorm for your Writing Task.

ANALYZE ▲

CREATE ▲

FOOD & DRINKS:
_____
_____
_____

WHERE:
_____
_____
_____

ACTIVITIES:
_____
_____
_____

NAME:
_____

WHEN:
_____
_____
_____

CLOTHES:
_____
_____
_____

SIMPLE SENTENCES 2

LANGUAGE

Objects and extra information

A simple sentence needs to have a *subject* and a *verb*. It must form a complete thought. The verb comes after the subject.

After the verb, there can be an *object* (usually a *noun* or *noun phrase*). You can also add extra information by using an *adjective* or a *prepositional phrase*.

subject	verb	noun phrase
I	visit	my family.

subject	verb	adjective
The people	are	happy.

subject	verb	prepositional phrase
The festival	is	in May.

PRISM **Online** Workbook

1   Underline the subject and circle the verb in each sentence.

   1   The children wear traditional clothes.
   2   My family and I watch the fireworks.
   3   I visit my aunt and uncle.
   4   People in the U.S. celebrate college graduation.
   5   My parents and I go downtown.

2   Underline the words that come after the verb in each sentence.
    Then write *N* for noun, *A* for adjective, and *P* for prepositional phrase.

   1   My family eats at home. _____
   2   The costumes are beautiful. _____
   3   We exchange presents. _____
   4   I celebrate in the evening. _____
   5   The festival is traditional. _____

3 Put the words in order to make complete sentences.

1 celebrate / People in Canada / Thanksgiving / .

   _____

2 on Sunday / My parents and I / cook / .

   _____

3 excited / is / Everyone in my town / about the party / .

   _____

4 eats / My family / in the morning / .

   _____

5 do not visit / my grandparents / We / .

   _____

LANGUAGE

Prepositional phrases

Sometimes a sentence can have an object and a prepositional phrase. The prepositional phrase comes after the object.

noun phrase (subject)	verb	noun phrase (object)	prepositional phrase
People in Mexico	eat	a special meal	in the evening.

The prepositional phrase can also come at the beginning of the sentence, followed by a comma.

prepositional phrase	noun phrase (subject)	verb	noun phrase (object)
In the evening,	people in Mexico	eat	a special meal.

4 Underline the prepositional phrase in each sentence. Circle the object.

1 We watch concerts at night.
2 In India, people celebrate the Magh Bihu festival.
3 People clean their homes in the morning.
4 Children have parties at school.
5 On Saturday, we watch the parades.

ORGANIZING SENTENCES INTO A PARAGRAPH

SKILLS

In written English, sentences are organized into paragraphs. A paragraph is a group of sentences about the same topic. A new topic should be put in a new paragraph.

A paragraph has a *topic sentence*, *supporting sentences*, and a *concluding sentence*. A paragraph is often written in this order:

1 The **topic sentence** describes what the paragraph is about. It is usually the first sentence in a paragraph.
2 The **supporting sentences** tell more about the topic and give details and examples. They are in the middle of the paragraph.
3 The **concluding sentence** ends the paragraph. It usually summarizes the main idea in the paragraph. The concluding sentence often starts with phrases like *In conclusion, In summary*, or *In sum*. Some short paragraphs do not have a concluding sentence.

PRISM Online Workbook

1 Look at the sentences. They are from two different paragraphs. Paragraph 1 is about a city. Paragraph 2 is about a festival. Organize the sentences into two paragraphs. Write *1* or *2* next to each sentence.

a Popfest is a music festival in the U.K. __2__
b It is a very noisy city. __1__
c People wear waterproof shoes and coats. _____
d In the summer, it is very hot. _____
e It happens in July. _____
f I live in Taipei. _____
g There are lots of shops and restaurants. _____
h People listen to music and dance. _____
i It's a great place to live. _____

2 Read the paragraph and follow the steps.

1 Circle the topic sentence and write *T* next to it.
2 Underline the supporting sentences and write *S* next to them.
3 Highlight the concluding sentence and write *C* next to it.

> When I was a child, my favorite day of the year was my birthday. I always went to the park with my family. My sister and brother gave me presents, and we usually played games. We ate lunch, and then for dessert, we ate the chocolate cake my mother made. In sum, I have very special memories of my birthday.

3 Read the sentences. Write *T* next to the topic sentence, *S* next to the supporting sentences, and *C* next to the concluding sentence.

   a Holi usually lasts for two days, and people laugh, have fun, and forget their troubles. _____

   b Holi is an ancient festival that celebrates the beginning of spring. _____

   c India celebrates the Festival of Colors, also known as Holi. _____

   d In conclusion, this festival is an interesting Indian celebration. _____

   e During this festival, friends and family get together and throw colored water and powder at each other – this activity celebrates the beautiful colors that come with spring. _____

4 Read the supporting sentences again. Circle the details and examples in the sentences that tell you more about the topic.

WRITING TASK

Describe a festival or special event.

PRISM Online Workbook

PLAN

1 Look at the idea map below. Use the information to complete the model paragraph on page 54.

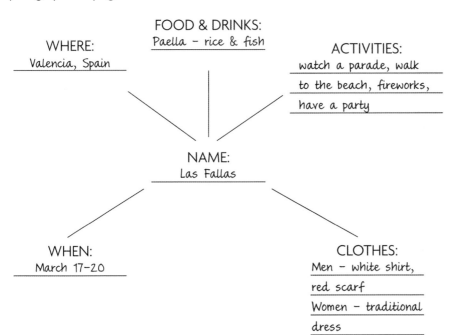

WHERE:
Valencia, Spain

FOOD & DRINKS:
Paella – rice & fish

ACTIVITIES:
watch a parade, walk to the beach, fireworks, have a party

NAME:
Las Fallas

WHEN:
March 17–20

CLOTHES:
Men – white shirt, red scarf
Women – traditional dress

In Valencia, Spain, people celebrate Las Fallas. Las Fallas is in the month of (1)_____ every year. It starts on the (2)_____ and ends on the 20th. People watch a (3)_____ in the streets. In the evening, everyone walks to the (4)_____ and has a party. There are fireworks. People also eat (5)_____ . It is a meal of (6)_____ and fish. Men wear a white shirt and a (7)_____ scarf and women wear traditional (8)_____ . In conclusion, Las Fallas is an enjoyable festival in Spain with fun activities, great food, and interesting traditional clothing.

2 Look back at the idea map you completed for Exercise 4 in Critical Thinking. Use your notes to write a topic sentence in the paragraph planner below. Write about the name of the event you chose and where it takes place.

Topic sentence: name and place	
Supporting sentence (1): when	
Supporting sentence (2): activities	
Supporting sentence (3): food and drinks	
Supporting sentence (4): clothes	
Concluding sentence	

3 Use your notes to write four supporting sentences about the details of the festival (e.g., when it takes place, activities, food and drinks, and clothes) in the planner.

4 Write your concluding sentence in the planner. Your concluding sentence should summarize the main idea of the paragraph.

5 Refer to the Task Checklist on page 55 as you prepare your paragraph.

WRITE A FIRST DRAFT

6 Use the sentences in the paragraph planner to write a paragraph.

REVISE

7 Use the Task Checklist to review your paragraph for content and structure.

TASK CHECKLIST	✔
Did you describe a festival or special event?	
Are the sentences organized in a paragraph?	
Does the paragraph start with a topic sentence stating the name of the event and where people celebrate it?	
Does the paragraph say when the event is?	
Does the paragraph have supporting sentences about the activities, food and drink, and clothes?	
Does the paragraph have a concluding sentence?	

8 Make any necessary changes to your paragraph.

EDIT

9 Use the Language Checklist to edit your paragraph for language errors.

LANGUAGE CHECKLIST	✔
Did you use *on*, *in*, and *at* correctly?	
Did you use adverbs of frequency correctly?	
Did you use correct sentence structure?	
Did you use prepositional phrases correctly?	

10 Make any necessary changes to your paragraph.

ON CAMPUS

CULTURAL EXCHANGE

Sometimes living in a different country with a new culture can be lonely. Students can find groups and activities to help them learn about the new culture, share their own culture, and meet new people.

PREPARING TO READ

1 Work with a partner. Discuss the questions.

1 Who do you hang out with after class? People from your culture? From other countries? From this country?
2 What language do you usually speak outside of class?
3 Do you ever do language exchanges with others? Why or why not?
4 What do you want to share with others about your culture?

WHILE READING

2 Read the flyer about a club on campus.

COME JOIN THE **NORTHSHORE COLLEGE** INTERCULTURE CLUB, A PLACE TO SHARE YOUR CULTURE AND LEARN ABOUT OTHERS.

Information meeting:

Monday, September 1, room 404 – Student Union.

Join us for these great fall events:

Interculture Club Meet and Greet

Come and meet other students for our weekly lunch and conversation. Sandwiches and drinks are provided. Every Wednesday in September, room 408. Open to all Northshore students. Bring ID.

Language Exchange

Practice English and teach your language. Every Thursday in September. Sign up online.

CultureFest

Friday, September 26, 12 to 5 p.m. Share your culture! Share your food, dance, photos, or anything from your country. Teach others about your home country. Sign up for a Culture Table for your cultural group. Or just come learn about other cultures.

Field Trip to Mount Rainier

Saturday, September 13. Vans leave at 8:30 a.m. Meet in front of the Art Museum. $45 for members / $55 for guests. Lunch is included. Sign up early. This is a popular trip!

3 Put the words and phrases in the correct box.

meets every week	free event	students teach something
must be a student	students travel by van	includes lunch
students must sign up	students must pay a fee	

Interculture Club Meet and Greet	Language Exchange	CultureFest	Mount Rainier Field Trip

PRACTICE

4 Work with a partner. Answer the questions about your interests for the Interculture Club membership. Share your interests with a partner.

NORTHSHORE COLLEGE INTERCULTURE CLUB
Membership Profile

Sharing Your Culture

- What would you like to teach others about your culture?
- What is one food or drink you would like to share from your country?
- What are three items from your culture that you would like to share?
- What are some places to share information about your culture?

Learning about New Cultures

- What other countries or cultures would you like to learn more about?
- What do you want to learn about?
- How do you want to learn those things?
- What are some places to learn more about other cultures?

REAL-WORLD APPLICATION

5 Work in small groups. Imagine creating your own cultural exchange meetup.

1. Discuss the details of your meetup group.
   a Decide on a group name and a focus for your meetup group.
   b Decide where you will meet and how often.
   c Describe what your group will do and who should join.
2. Design a flyer for your meetup group.
3. Share your flyer with the class. Which flyer is best?

THE INTERNET AND TECHNOLOGY

ACTIVATE YOUR KNOWLEDGE

Look at the photo and answer the questions.

1 What do you think the man's job is?
2 What is he using the tablet for?
3 How much time do you spend on the Internet every week?
4 What activities do you use the Internet for?

PREPARING TO WATCH

ACTIVATING YOUR KNOWLEDGE

1 Work with a partner and answer the questions.

1 Why do people buy things from websites?
2 What kind of advertisements or commercials do you see online?
3 Do you ever worry when you use technology? Why or why not?

USING YOUR KNOWLEDGE

2 Read the opinion. Do you agree or disagree? Discuss your answer with your partner.

> People should never give personal information when they are online in public places such as airports, hotels, or coffee shops.

GLOSSARY

habit (n) something that you do regularly, almost without thinking about it

advertising (n) the business of trying to persuade people to buy products or services

ad (n) an advertisement; a picture, short video, song, etc. that tries to get you to buy a product or service

predict (v) to say what you think will happen in the future

clue (n) a sign or piece of information that helps you solve a problem or answer a question

WHILE WATCHING

3 ▶ Watch the video. Complete each sentence with a word from the box.

looking   taking   talking   texting   showing   walking

1 A woman is _____ someone on her phone.
2 A man is _____ to someone on his phone.
3 People are _____ while _____ at their phones.
4 A woman is _____ a picture with her camera.
5 A computer is _____ an ad on a website.

4 ▶ Watch again. Circle the correct answers.

1 The amount of data is growing by 2.5 *million / billion* gigabytes every day.
2 All that data is worth a lot of *money / time*.
3 Mike Baker decided to help change the world of *traveling / advertising*.
4 Companies could predict what people might want to *buy / sell*.
5 Mike's program looks at data *quickly / slowly*.
6 Personalized ads are sent to *companies / customers*.

5 Match the sentence halves. Compare your answers with a partner.

1 The amount of data is growing because _____
2 Using data is difficult because _____
3 Mike Baker found a partner because _____
4 You can't get away from ads completely because _____
5 Mike hunts data because _____

a he needed help.
b there is too much of it.
c we leave information every time we call, text, or search online.
d it is worth a lot of money.
e we live in a world of personalized ads.

6 Work with a partner. The speaker in the video says, "Maybe it's better to see ads for things you like than for things you don't care about." What does he mean?

DISCUSSION

7 Work in small groups. Discuss the questions.

1 What are some differences between ads on TV, in newspapers or magazines, and online?
2 What kinds of ads do you prefer to see on your phone or computer?
3 Name five companies that advertise around the world. Describe one ad that you remember.

READING

PREPARING TO READ

UNDERSTANDING KEY VOCABULARY

1 Read the sentences and write the words in bold next to the definitions.

1 People should always use a **secret** password on their smartphone. This helps to keep their information safe.

2 After I buy the correct **software**, I'll be able to make music and draw pictures on my computer.

3 Sarah has an **interest** in the newest technology, so she always learns about it very quickly.

4 A lot of websites **collect** information about the people who look at them.

5 Shopping websites must have strong **security**. People have to be sure their personal information and credit card numbers are safe.

6 Ahmed likes to **record** his friends when they do something funny. Then he shares the videos online.

7 One **benefit** of tablets is that they are small, so they are easy to take anywhere with you.

8 Many people don't want to pay to use news websites because so much of the news is already **free** online.

a _____ (n) a good or helpful result or effect

b _____ (n) something you enjoy doing or learning about

c _____ (v) to get things from different places and bring them together

d _____ (adj) costing no money

e _____ (n) the things that are done to keep someone or something safe

f _____ (v) to store sounds, pictures, or information on a camera or computer so that they can be used in the future

g _____ (n) programs you use to make a computer do different things

h _____ (adj) not known or seen by other people

SCANNING TO PREDICT CONTENT

2 Before you read, circle the title and subtitle in the Web page on page 63.

3 Circle the best description of the topic of the Web page.

a the benefits (+) of the Internet

b the dangers (–) of the Internet

c why people use the Internet

4 Read the Web page and check your answers.

Someone's Always Watching You Online …

1 Did you know that when you surf the Web, many websites put **secret software** on your computer? The software **collects** a large amount of information about you and sends it to Internet companies. The Internet companies sell it to other businesses. Your personal information can also be gathered from social media sites. There are many ways your information can be used.

2 First, companies collect your information. The companies find out where you live, what websites you visit, and what you do online. With this information, they can guess other things about you. For example, they can guess if you are male[1] or female[2], how old you are, and your **interests**. The companies use this information to decide which advertisements are best for you. Two people can go to the same website, but they will see different ads. For example, someone who likes sports could see an ad for sneakers, and someone who likes films might see an ad for a movie.

3 Your personal information could also be sold. Some companies collect information just so they can sell it to other businesses. A business that collects and sells personal information is called a *data broker*. When data brokers sell your information, a lot of different companies will know your online habits. Then these companies will advertise products or other websites to you.

4 Another way your personal information can be collected is through social media. When your information is on social media, a lot of people can see it. Even if you don't use social media, a friend might post a picture or video of you with your name on it. Pictures and videos can be shared for **free** on social media, which is one of the great **benefits**. However, that same act of sharing could be a problem for your own **security**. If someone knows too much about you, they can steal your identity. Then they can buy things online and post messages while pretending to be you.

5 All of your online habits can be **recorded**. Studying people's online habits is big business. Your personal information is very valuable to companies. That is how they know who to send their ads to. The Internet reaches almost every corner of the world, but the danger is that your personal information might travel that far, too.

find out more

[1]**male** (adj) a man
[2]**female** (adj) a woman

WHILE READING

Reading for main ideas

When reading, it is important to understand the main ideas in the text. Remember that each paragraph has one topic. The main idea of a paragraph is the most important point of what the author says about the topic. The main idea can often be found in the topic sentence, which is usually the first or second sentence in the paragraph.

READING FOR MAIN IDEAS

PRISM Online Workbook

READING FOR DETAILS

5 Read the text again. Circle the correct ending for each sentence.

1 Internet companies *ask you for information / take information without asking you.*

2 Internet companies show *different advertisements to different people / the same advertisements to everyone.*

6 Write the words from the box in the correct place in the table. For some items, more than one answer is possible.

> your address   your interests   your social media page
> other websites you might like
> your online habits   your gender (male/female)   a data broker
> your age   the websites you visit

A What do Internet companies find out about you?	B What do Internet companies guess about you?	C What do Internet companies decide?	D How do Internet companies find out about you?

READING BETWEEN THE LINES

SKILLS

Making inferences

When people read, they often make inferences about a text. To make an inference, think about what the author writes, the way they write it, and what you already know about the subject to make a guess about information that isn't in the text. Inferences are not facts, so different answers are often possible.

7 Look at the advertisements on the Web page. What can you guess about the person using the website?

MAKING INFERENCES

PRISM Online Workbook

   1 How old is the reader?
   2 What are the reader's interests?

8 What can you infer from the text? Circle the correct answers.

   a You can ask companies to stop selling your information.
   b You don't know what websites are collecting information about you.
   c You should be extra careful with your personal information when you travel.
   d Someone could pretend to be you and send an email to your friend.
   e Data brokers probably make a lot of money selling personal information.

9 Work with a partner. Compare and discuss your answers.

DISCUSSION

10 Read the three opinions about the topic of the Web page. Circle the opinion you agree with most.

   a I don't think companies should take any of this information from you—it's really bad. Think about the danger of so many people knowing your private information.

   b I don't see the problem. Companies need to make money somehow—we get a lot of free things on the Internet, and this is a good way to pay for them. There are benefits for everyone.

   c I think it's great. If companies can show you advertisements for things you like, you can find out about new things.

11 Work with a partner. Compare and discuss your answers.

PREPARING TO READ

UNDERSTANDING
KEY VOCABULARY

PRISM Online
Workbook

1 Read the definitions. Complete the sentences with the correct form of the words in bold.

> **affect** (v) to influence someone or something; to cause change
> **creative** (adj) good at thinking of new ideas or creating new and unusual things
> **download** (v) to copy computer programs, music, or other information electronically from the Internet to your computer
> **educational** (adj) providing education, or relating to education
> **imagination** (n) the part of your mind that creates ideas or pictures of things that are not real or that you have not seen
> **improve** (v) to get better or to make something better

1 There are a lot of apps you can _____ onto your phone to help you learn a new language.
2 I like to watch _____ videos so I can learn something new. I just watched one about the history of airplanes.
3 Gabriela took a class to _____ her computer skills. Now she can type faster and find information on the Internet more easily.
4 Reading, telling stories, and having new adventures can help kids to develop their _____ .
5 Art students are very _____ . In my program, they use new software to make some really interesting and beautiful designs.
6 Spending too much time on your smartphone may _____ your health in negative ways. It can hurt your eyes and give you a headache.

2 Write the words from the box in the correct place in the table.

> advantage   disadvantage   benefit   negative   positive

+	−

USING YOUR
KNOWLEDGE

3 Discuss the questions with a partner.

1 Why do some people like video games?
2 What ages do you think most video game players are?

Video Games for Kids: Win or Lose?

1   Do video games **affect** our children negatively? Today, our children spend more and more time online. Many children spend a lot of their free time playing games on the Internet, on video game systems, or on their mobile devices. In the U.S., 97% of teenagers play video games every week, and children as young as five play video games regularly. This information tells us that the benefits and dangers of video games must be carefully considered.

2   For many people, video games are fun and **educational**. They have bright lights, funny cartoons, and exciting stories. Everywhere you look, you can see children playing these games. They play on buses and trains, in restaurants, and even at school. Video games also make you think in a **creative** way, and you have to move your hands and eyes quickly. This can **improve** the way that a child's brain works. Video games also make children use their **imagination**. The player has to do many creative things, like draw, tell stories, and build things. Video games are also a good way to teach children about technology because they can learn how computers and other devices work while they play.

3   However, a recent study suggests that video games can also be bad for children. First, children can **download** many games for free. They don't need money, so they don't need to ask their parents if they can download the games. This means that parents often don't know if their children are playing violent or scary games. Second, many children spend too much time playing games on computers, smartphones, and tablets, and this can lead to health problems—children who spend too much time on the computer and don't exercise can become overweight[1]. Third, if children spend too much time playing games instead of doing homework, they can have problems at school and get bad grades. Finally, video games can affect children's social skills. Playing and working with friends is very important for children, and it teaches them how to talk to other people. If children spend too much time playing video games by themselves, they might not learn how to play with their friends.

4   In conclusion, it seems clear that video games have some advantages and some disadvantages. On the one hand, they are fun and have many educational benefits for children. On the other hand, they can cause problems with children's health and social skills. It is up to parents to know what games their children are playing and how much time they spend on them. Parents should also make sure their children get enough exercise and spend time with other children.

[1]**overweight** (adj) too heavy or weighing more than the normal amount

WHILE READING

4 Read the essay on page 67. Write the paragraph numbers that include the main ideas below. Then write the sentences from the text that contain each main idea.

4 Read the essay on page 67. Write the paragraph numbers that include the main ideas below. Then write the sentences from the text that contain each main idea.

1 Video games have some disadvantages. Paragraph: _____
   Sentence: _____

2 Video games have some advantages. Paragraph: _____
   Sentence: _____

5 Cross out the advantages and disadvantages in the table that are not mentioned in the text.

+	−
Video games ... 1 are creative. 2 improve the way children think. 3 teach children about money. 4 are fun. 5 can help children exercise.	Video games ... 6 can cause health problems. 7 are boring. 8 can make it difficult for children to learn to talk to people. 9 can be unsuitable for children. 10 can cause problems between parents and children.

READING BETWEEN THE LINES

6 Read the questions. Circle the correct answer. Compare your answers with a partner.

1 What type of text is this?
   a an essay
   b a newspaper article
   c a website

2 Who do you think is the author?
   a a parent
   b a journalist
   c a student

DISCUSSION

7 Work with a partner. Answer the questions.

1 Do you think that video games are bad for children? Why or why not?
2 Do you think spending a lot of time on the Internet is good or bad for you?
3 Use information from Reading 1 and Reading 2 to answer the following questions. What are some of your online habits? What might an Internet company infer about you from your online habits?

COMPOUND NOUNS

In English, two or more words can be put together to form a new word.

A *compound noun* is a noun that is made up of two or three different words. Compound nouns are very common in English. Some compound nouns are written as one word. Others are written as two or three separate words.

A **laptop** is a small computer that you can carry around with you.

A **touch screen** is a screen on a computer, smartphone, or tablet that you touch in order to give it instructions.

A **password** is a secret word that allows you to use your computer.

A **homepage** is the first page you see when you look at the Internet.

PRISM Online Workbook

1 Match the compound nouns to their definitions.

1	video game	**a**	a page of information on the Internet
2	computer program	**b**	a set of keys that you use to type
3	keyboard	**c**	a phone that can be used as a computer
4	email address	**d**	a game that is played on a screen
5	Web page	**e**	instructions that make a computer do something
6	smartphone	**f**	an address for an email inbox

2 Use the compound nouns from Exercise 1 to complete the sentences.

1 My computer's _____ is broken. I can only type in capital letters.

2 I just bought a new _____ . I can use the Internet anywhere now.

3 What's your _____ ? I'll send you the pictures from the party.

4 I found a(n) _____ with good information I can use for my essay.

5 I can play this _____ on my computer or on my smartphone. It's really fun!

6 I downloaded a(n) _____ to check my computer for viruses.

GIVING OPINIONS

In academic writing, use the phrases *I think that*, *I believe that*, *It seems to me that*, and *In my opinion* to talk about your opinions.

Opinion: *Video games are bad for children.*

I think that video games are bad for children.
I believe that video games are bad for children.
It seems to me that video games are bad for children.
In my opinion, video games are bad for children.

PRISM Online Workbook

3 Look at the phrases for giving opinions. Which phrase needs a comma at the end of it?

   a I think that
   b I believe that
   c It seems to me that
   d In my opinion

4 Complete the sentences with an adjective. Write sentences that are true for you.

   1 Video games are _____ .
   2 Online shopping is _____ .
   3 Social media sites are _____ .
   4 Online banking is _____ .
   5 Smartphones are _____ .
   6 Watching videos online is _____ .

5 Rewrite the sentences in Exercise 4 to show that they are your opinion. Use the phrases in the box above.

   1 _____
   2 _____
   3 _____
   4 _____
   5 _____
   6 _____

WRITING

CRITICAL THINKING

At the end of this unit, you will write an opinion paragraph. Look at this unit's Writing Task below.

 The Internet wastes our time. It does not help us do more work. Do you agree or disagree?

Analyzing a question

Before you answer a question, it is important to analyze exactly what the question asks you to do. You can then decide what to write in order to answer the question correctly.

1 Match each question to the correct way to answer it.

ANALYZE ▲

1 How does the Internet waste our time? How does it help us do more work? _____

2 The Internet wastes our time more than it helps us do work. Do you agree or disagree? _____

a Give your opinion about whether the Internet wastes our time or helps us do more work. Give examples to support your argument.

b Describe the ways the Internet wastes our time and the ways it helps us do more work.

2 Look at the advantages and disadvantages of the Internet in the box. Write them in the correct place in the table on page 72.

> You can get help from different websites.
> You could lose valuable information if your computer breaks.
> You can visit social media sites.
> You can read newspapers from around the world.
> People can work at home sometimes.
> You can play video games.
> You can read your email.
> You can watch educational videos.
> You could get addicted to technology.
> You can learn new words in a different language.

computers help us do work	computers waste our time

3 Work with a partner. Add two more points to each column.

4 Which points are the most convincing? Why?

 EVALUATE

GRAMMAR FOR WRITING

CONNECTING IDEAS

LANGUAGE

And, also, and *too*

Use the coordinating conjunction *and* or the adverbs *also* or *too* to add information. Connecting ideas makes your writing better and easier to understand.

Use *and* to join two ideas in a single sentence.
My sister has a computer. She has a smartphone.
→ My sister has a computer **and** a smartphone.

Jessica texts her friends. She shares photos.
→ Jessica texts her friends **and** shares photos.

You can use *also* and *too* to connect the ideas in two separate sentences.
My sister uses her computer a lot. She **also** has a smartphone.
My sister uses her computer a lot. She has a smartphone, **too**.

Put *also* before the main verb. Put *too* at the end of the sentence and put a comma before it.

1 Join each pair of sentences to make one simple sentence with *and*.

1 Video games are boring. They are bad for children.
  Video games are boring and bad for children.

2 You can share photos. You can talk to your friends.

3 I use online banking. I check my email.

4 She does homework on her computer. She watches movies
  on her computer.

5 I often shop for clothes on the Internet. I pay with my credit card.

2 Look at the sentence pairs. Rewrite the sentences with *also* or *too* in the
second sentence to connect the ideas.

1 Many people download music. They download videos. (also)

2 I write a blog about traveling. I read a lot of travel blogs. (too)

3 I read the newspapers online. I check social media. (also)

4 I look at maps on my phone. I look at photos on my phone. (also)

LANGUAGE

Compound sentences

A *compound sentence* contains two independent clauses (complete thoughts).
Each clause has its own subject and verb. Use a *coordinating conjunction*
(*and* or *but*) to link two complete thoughts.

Use *and* to add information.
Lina doesn't have a smartphone. She doesn't want one.
→ Lina doesn't have a smartphone, **and** she doesn't want one.

Use *but* to give contrasting or different information or ideas.
Martin reads books on a tablet. Jose likes to read printed books.
→ Martin reads books on a tablet, **but** Jose likes to read printed books.

Use a comma before a coordinating conjunction in a compound sentence.

3 Join each pair of simple sentences to make one compound sentence. Use *and* or *but*.

1 Video games are boring. They can affect your social skills.
   Video games are boring, and they can affect your social skills.

2 I sent an email to Alan. He did not write me back.
   _____

3 I like to shop online. My father thinks it's not safe.
   _____

4 I call my mother every Saturday. I visit her every Sunday.
   _____

5 I bought a new phone. It doesn't work.
   _____

6 You can check the weather. You can find a good restaurant.
   _____

7 Some games are educational. Other games are just for fun.
   _____

However

You can also connect two sentences with contrasting or different information or ideas with *however*.

Smartphones are very popular. They are very expensive.
→ Smartphones are very popular. **However,** they are very expensive.

Use *however* at the start of a new sentence, followed by a comma.

4 Rewrite each pair of sentences. First write a compound sentence using *but*. Then link the ideas with *however*.

1 The Internet is very useful. It can be dangerous.
   a _The Internet is very useful, but it can be dangerous._
   b _The Internet is very useful. However, it can be dangerous._

2 Many apps are fun. Some apps are a waste of time.
   a _____
   b _____

3 I use online banking. I sometimes forget my password.
   a _____
   b _____

4 I use the Internet on my smartphone. Sometimes it is very slow.
   a _____
   b _____

ACADEMIC WRITING SKILLS

TOPIC SENTENCES

The topic sentence tells you the main idea of a paragraph. It is usually the first or second sentence in a paragraph. A topic sentence has two parts: the *topic* and the *controlling idea*. The topic tells what the paragraph is about. The controlling idea gives the topic a focus.

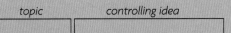

    topic   *controlling idea*

The Internet has many advantages. You can find information quickly and keep in touch with your friends. It's also easy to share photos and watch videos. The Internet makes life easier.

1 Look at paragraphs 2 and 3 in Reading 2 on page 67. Underline the topic sentences.

2 Read the topic sentences. Underline the topic. Circle the controlling idea.

  1 Social media sites make it easy to keep in touch with your friends.
  2 Smartphones can be expensive.
  3 Information on the Internet is not reliable.
  4 You can access information online from all over the world.

3 In each paragraph, the topic sentence is missing. Write the topic sentences from Exercise 2 above the correct paragraph.

a _____

It is easy to spend a lot of money on them. Contracts for the phones can also cost a lot of money. It is important to be careful and pay attention to what you spend.

b _____

You can read newspapers, magazines, and blogs from many different countries. You can even translate information from other languages using a translation website. It is easy to find out what is happening anywhere you want.

c _____

You can look at your friends' photos and see what they are doing. Your friends can send you messages and links. You can also share interesting articles and videos.

d _____

Anyone can publish articles and information online. Websites often do not say who wrote an article or where they got their facts. People can write things that are not true.

The Internet wastes our time. It does not help us do more work.
Do you agree or disagree?

PLAN

1 Look at the question above. Do you agree or disagree?

2 Look at the table in Critical Thinking. Highlight the three ideas that best support your opinion.

3 Look at the paragraph planner.

   1 Write your topic sentence in the planner.
   2 Write your three supporting ideas in the planner.

Topic sentence:

Supporting idea 1:

Supporting idea 2:

Supporting idea 3:

4 Refer to the Task Checklist on page 77 as you prepare your paragraph.

WRITE A FIRST DRAFT

5 Write the first draft of your paragraph. Connect your ideas and sentences.

REVISE

6 Use the Task Checklist to review your paragraph for content and structure.

TASK CHECKLIST	✔
Did you include a topic sentence with a controlling idea?	
Did you give your opinion on the topic?	
Did you include three supporting ideas?	
Did you include a concluding sentence?	

7 Make any necessary changes to your paragraph.

EDIT

8 Use the Language Checklist to edit your paragraph for language errors.

LANGUAGE CHECKLIST	✔
Did you use compound nouns correctly?	
Did you use the correct sentence order with the phrases *I think that*, *I believe that*, *it seems to me that*, and *in my opinion*?	
Did you use *and, also,* and *too* correctly?	
Did you use *but* and *however* correctly?	
Did you use compound sentences?	

9 Make any necessary changes to your paragraph.

ON CAMPUS

THE VIRTUAL CLASSROOM

SKILLS

For many college classes, students have to do some work online. Professors expect students to be active both online and in class. Online participation is often part of a student's grade.

PREPARING TO READ

1 Work with a partner. Discuss the questions.

1 What do you do online for your classes?
2 How do you feel about online discussions? Why?
3 Do you prefer an online class or a face-to-face class? Why?
4 What are the advantages of online projects and discussions?

WHILE READING

2 Read part of a syllabus from a sociology class.

CLASS WEBSITE

For this class, students can find lecture notes and articles on the class website. Students will also use the class website to do the following tasks: submit[1] homework, take quizzes, do group projects, and post[2] responses for weekly discussions. Students should do the following:

- check the website each Monday for updates and assignments
- complete all tasks on time
- contact the professor by email if there is a problem

WEEKLY ONLINE DISCUSSIONS

Each Monday, a new question will be posted on the online discussion board. The discussion is open until Friday at 5 p.m. Students must actively participate in the discussion every week.

This part of the course counts for 25% of the final grade.

Students must do the following:

1 Post an answer to the question every week. Answers should be 30–40 words. Please post an answer on Monday or Tuesday.

2 Respond to two classmates' answers. Responses should be 20–30 words.

All discussions should:

- be about the topic
- use complete sentences in paragraphs
- use academic language
- use correct spelling
- use good grammar
- be respectful of others

[1]**submit** (v) turn in, either online or to someone
[2]**post** (v) put on a website for others to see

3 Write *T* (true) or *F* (false) next to the statements.

_____ 1 The professor will post notes from the class lecture.

_____ 2 Students can use informal language in an online discussion.

_____ 3 Students can post a response on Saturday.

_____ 4 Homework should be given to the professor.

_____ 5 Students should check their spelling and grammar.

PRACTICE

4 Work with a partner. Read the discussion question and the answer.
Match the responses to the descriptions.

a good response

b too short

c not academic language

d not about the topic

Question: Is social media a good way to meet people?

Answer: Posted by Kyle Mapes, January 12 at 10:03 p.m.

Social media is a great way to meet people. Students can find a study group. They can also find people for a carpool. They can meet people with the same interests, too. [32 words]

_____ **Response 1**: Posted by Angela Guerra, January 13 at 9:45 a.m.

I agree with you, Kyle. However, social media can be dangerous, too. Students should be careful online. Also, parents should always help young children. [24 words]

_____ **Response 2**: Posted by Gitta Haagen, January 13 at 11:00 a.m.

Yeah, Kyle. Social media is awesome. You know, a lot of people meet that way. Like me and my friends. [20 words]

_____ **Response 3**: Posted by Andre Guterson, January 13 at 12:20 p.m.

Facebook is not very popular now. I think more people use Instagram and Snapchat. WhatsApp is also a good choice for international students. [23 words]

_____ **Response 4**: Posted by Ayse Aydin, January 16 at 4:45 p.m.

Social media has advantages and disadvantages. It's both positive and negative. [11 words]

REAL-WORLD APPLICATION

5 Read the question and the student answer. Write a response.

Question: Which is better for learning: an online discussion board or a classroom discussion?

Answer: Posted by Yoshi Sasaki, March 15 at 2:45 p.m.

Online discussion boards are better because students can think about their ideas. Some international students don't like to talk in class. However, they are more comfortable online. Students will learn more if they are not nervous. [36 words]

6 Discuss your written response with a partner.

LEARNING OBJECTIVES

Reading skills	Read for details; use your knowledge to predict content
Grammar	Comparative and superlative adjectives
Academic writing skills	Supporting sentences; giving examples
Writing Task	Write a descriptive paragraph
On Campus	See a doctor

WEATHER AND CLIMATE

ACTIVATE YOUR KNOWLEDGE

1 Match the types of weather to the photos.

| snow (n) | sun (n) | rain (n) | wind (n) |

2 What is your favorite type of weather? Why?

3 What is your least favorite type of weather? Why?

4 Look at the large photo. What type of weather do you see?

WATCH AND LISTEN

PREPARING TO WATCH

ACTIVATING YOUR
KNOWLEDGE

1 Work with a partner and answer the questions.

1 What is a thunderstorm?
2 Why are some people afraid of thunderstorms?
3 How can wind from a storm be dangerous?

PREDICTING CONTENT
USING VISUALS

2 Look at the pictures from the video. Discuss the questions with your partner.

1 What do you think the video is about?
2 Where do you think it takes place?
3 What do you think is the man's job?

> **GLOSSARY**
>
> **extreme** (adj) the worst or most serious; for example, extreme weather conditions
>
> **tornado** (n) an extremely strong, dangerous wind that blows in a circle
>
> **alley** (n) a narrow street between buildings
>
> **produce** (v) to cause a reaction or a result
>
> **Doppler radar** (n) a special radar system that can give us information about a storm
>
> **spin** (v) if something spins, it turns around and around quickly

WHILE WATCHING

UNDERSTANDING
DETAILS

3 ▶ Watch the video. Circle the correct answers.

1 The middle of the United States is called Tornado *Alley* / *Valley*.
2 The year *2010* / *2011* was very bad for tornadoes.
3 That year a dangerous tornado killed more than *160* / *60* people.
4 Scientists *can* / *cannot* predict when and where tornadoes will happen.
5 Josh Wurman is a *computer* / *weather* scientist.
6 *Seventy-five* / *twenty-five* percent of thunderstorms produce tornadoes.
7 Finding the right thunderstorm is *easy* / *difficult*.

4 ▶ Watch again. Match the questions to the correct answers.

1 What does spring bring?   **a** Tornadoes.
2 What killed people in Joplin, Missouri?   **b** Warm, wet air.
3 What is Josh Wurman studying?   **c** A dangerous tornado.
4 What does Josh use to find storms?   **d** Tornadoes happen quickly.
5 Why did the team have to move fast?   **e** A Doppler radar scanner.

UNDERSTANDING
MAIN IDEAS

5 Read the statements. What is the video mainly about?
Circle the best answer.

a Some thunderstorms produce tornadoes, but others do not.
b Tornadoes are one of the most dangerous kinds of weather in the world.
c The winds in a tornado can spin faster than the winds in a hurricane.

MAKING INFERENCES

6 Work with a partner. Do Josh and his team enjoy their work?
How do you know?

DISCUSSION

7 Work with a partner. Discuss the questions.

1 Is Josh Wurman's job important? Why or why not?
2 What other jobs are related to weather?
3 Why do people choose to live in areas with extreme weather?

8 Work in small groups. Make a list of five things you would do to prepare for a tornado.

READING

PREPARING TO READ

1 You are going to read a text about extreme weather. Before you read, look at the definitions. Complete the sentences with the correct form of the words in bold.

> **almost** (adv) not everything, but very close to it
> **cover** (v) to lie on the surface of something
> **dangerous** (adj) can harm or hurt someone or something
> **huge** (adj) extremely large in size or amount
> **last** (v) to continue for a period of time
> **lightning** (n) a flash of bright light in the sky during a storm
> **thunder** (n) the sudden loud noise that comes after a flash of lightning

1 I think the big snow storm will _____ the ground in snow. We won't be able to see any grass at all.
2 Although _____ can be very scary, it is also beautiful when it flashes in the sky.
3 _____ every house on our street was destroyed by the fire. Only two houses were saved.
4 Asli got sick when the weather changed. Luckily, it didn't _____ long. She felt better after a couple of days.
5 The _____ scared our cats. They wouldn't come out from under the bed until the storm ended and it was quiet again.
6 There has been a _____ increase in rainfall this year. As a result, the lakes and rivers are at the highest levels in years.
7 Swimming in the rain can be fun, but it's _____ if there is lightning. You should get out of the water right away so you don't get hurt.

2 Work with a partner and discuss the questions.

1 What kind of weather do you have in your town or city?
2 What does the word *extreme* mean?
3 What is an example of extreme weather?

1 Extreme weather

Extreme weather is when the weather is very different from normal. Extreme weather can take place over an hour, a day, or a long period of time. It can be **dangerous**, and in some cases, it can cause natural disasters[1].

2 Hurricanes

A hurricane is a type of storm. These storms are also called cyclones or typhoons. In North America and Central America, they are called hurricanes; in the North Pacific, they are called typhoons; and in the Indian Ocean and South Pacific, they are called cyclones. These storms are **huge**—they can be over 300 miles (500 kilometers) wide. They start over the ocean and move toward land. When they come to land, they bring **thunder**, **lightning**, strong winds, and very heavy rain. They can be very dangerous and destroy buildings, and even kill people.

3 Heat waves and droughts

A heat wave is when there are high temperatures and it is much hotter than normal. In many areas, heat waves are not a problem. However, in parts of the U.S., temperatures may reach above 120 °F (49 °C) in a heat wave, and **last** for a few days or several months. And in some places such as California, heat waves can cause droughts[2]. In a drought, there is not enough water for farmers to grow food. In some cases, people die because they don't have enough water to drink. Droughts are common in many countries in Africa, but in the last ten years, droughts also happened in Afghanistan, China, and Iran.

4 Rainstorms

Too much rain can cause floods[3]. Floods can destroy buildings and kill people. They can also destroy plants and food, which can mean that there is not enough food for people to eat. In 2015, there were very bad floods in South America. In Argentina, the Paraguay River was **almost** 50 feet (15 meters) higher than normal, and water **covered** the streets. In Paraguay, hundreds of thousands of people had to leave their homes. Strong winds damaged the power lines, and several people died. It was the worst flood in 50 years.

5 Sandstorms

A sandstorm is a large storm of dust and sand with strong winds. Sandstorms can be very dangerous. It is difficult to travel by car because people can't see anything. Even walking can be difficult. Sandstorms are common in the Middle East and in China. One of the worst sandstorms was in Iraq in 2011 when a storm lasted a whole week, causing many people to have breathing problems.

[1]**disaster** (n) an event that causes a lot of harm or damage
[2]**drought** (n) a long period when there is no rain and people do not have enough water
[3]**flood** (n) if a place floods or is flooded, it becomes covered in water

WHILE READING

3 Read the text. Then circle the statement that contains the most important idea in each paragraph.

1 Paragraph 1
   a Extreme weather is unusual and can cause natural disasters.
   b Extreme weather can take place over a short time or a long time.
2 Paragraph 2
   a Hurricanes cover a very wide area.
   b Hurricanes are huge, dangerous storms.
3 Paragraph 3
   a In a heat wave, temperatures are hotter than normal.
   b Heat waves sometimes occur in the U.S.
4 Paragraph 4
   a In 2015, there were floods in South America.
   b Floods happen when there is too much rain.
5 Paragraph 5
   a A sandstorm is a storm with a lot of wind and dust.
   b Certain countries have frequent sandstorms.

Reading for details

When reading a text, it is important to understand the details as well as the main ideas. Details give specific information about the main ideas. You can find details in a text by looking for key words. Read the sentences with the key words carefully to understand important information.

READING FOR DETAILS

PRISM Online Workbook

4 Circle the correct ending for each sentence.

1 Hurricanes move from ...
   a land to sea.
   b sea to land.
2 Heat waves ...
   a may lead to droughts.
   b aren't usually a big problem.
3 Paraguay had ...
   a a very big flood in 2015.
   b no food for people to eat in 2015.
4 In 2011, ...
   a China had a bad sandstorm.
   b Iraq had a bad sandstorm.

READING BETWEEN THE LINES

**RECOGNIZING
TEXT TYPE**

5 Circle the correct answer.

1 What type of text is this?
   a an excerpt from a newspaper   b an excerpt from a textbook
2 Who would be interested in reading this text?
   a someone studying biology   b someone studying climate
3 What kind of information is included in the text?
   a facts   b opinions

DISCUSSION

6 Discuss the questions with a partner.

1 Do you prefer hot or cold weather?
2 What is the worst weather you have experienced?
3 Has the weather in your country changed in recent years?

READING 2

PREPARING TO READ

1 You are going to read about the Sahara Desert. Before you read, try to answer the questions.

USING YOUR KNOWLEDGE

PRISM Online Workbook

1 Where is the Sahara Desert?
  a South Africa
  b North Africa
  c Central Asia

2 What is the weather like there?
  a hot and dry
  b cold and wet
  c hot and wet

2 Read the sentences. Write the words in bold next to the definitions.

UNDERSTANDING KEY VOCABULARY

PRISM Online Workbook

1 It was hot and sunny all day, so it was a **shock** when it suddenly started to rain.
2 The temperature will **rise** over the summer months. It will get hotter every day.
3 Let's wait and see what the weather is like tomorrow. Then we'll **decide** if we want to go to the beach or to a museum.
4 Be **careful** when you drive on icy roads. Go slowly and watch out for other cars.
5 Lloró, Colombia has the most **precipitation** in the world. It gets about 41.6 feet (12.7 meters) of rain every year.
6 The temperature might **drop**, so we'll build a fire to stay warm.

a _____ (adj) paying attention to what you are doing so that you do not have an accident, make a mistake, or damage something
b _____ (v) to decrease; to fall or go down
c _____ (v) to choose between one possibility or another
d _____ (n) a big, unpleasant surprise
e _____ (v) to increase; to go up
f _____ (n) rain or snow that falls to the ground

3 Read the article on page 89 and check your answers to Exercise 1.

WHILE READING

READING FOR
MAIN IDEAS

4 Write the paragraph numbers next to the best titles.

a Stay out of the Sun _____
b Drink Water _____
c Stay Cool During the Day and Warm at Night _____
d Don't Eat Too Much _____
e Stay with Your Car _____

READING FOR DETAILS

5 Match the sentence halves. Use the graph on page 89 and information in paragraph 2 to help you.

1 The coldest time is
2 The average amount of rain in a year
3 The temperature is 91 °F (33 °C)
4 The coldest temperature at night

a between 2 p.m. and 4 p.m.
b is 30 °F (-1 °C).
c is 3 inches (70 mm).
d at four o'clock in the morning.

READING BETWEEN THE LINES

6 Where might you find an article like this?

a in a newspaper
b in a travel magazine
c in a math textbook

DISCUSSION

7 Look at the list. Which things would you like most if you were alone in the desert? Choose the three most important things.

a a blanket
b a mirror
c five gallons (19 liters) of water
d a radio
e a map
f a hat

8 Work with a partner. Compare your answers and explain your choices.

9 Work with a partner. Choose three extreme weather situations from Reading 1. Discuss some survival tips for the extreme weather you chose.

RECOGNIZING
TEXT TYPE

SYNTHESIZING

Surviving[1] the Sea of Sand
How to Stay Alive in the Sahara Desert

Brad Rogers

1 Can you imagine a sea of sand three times bigger than India? This is the Sahara Desert, the largest desert in the world. It covers 11 countries in North Africa and is over 3 million square miles (9 million square kilometers). That's more than 25% of Africa.

2 In the Sahara, temperatures are very different during the day and at night. It is much hotter during the day than at night. During the day, the hottest time is between 2 p.m. and 4 p.m., when temperatures **rise** to 91 °F (33 °C). But it is very cold at night—the coldest time is at 4 a.m., when temperatures fall to 30 °F (-1 °C). The Sahara is very dry. The average **precipitation** in a year is only 3 inches (70 millimeters).

3 Because of the extreme temperatures in the desert, it is a very difficult place to survive. Marco Rivera, our survival expert, has some tips.

4 Take warm clothes and a blanket. You will need a hat, long pants, and a wool sweater to keep you warm at night. During the day, cover your body, head, and face. Clothes protect you from the sun and keep water in your body. You will also need a warm blanket at night. It can get cold very quickly. When the temperature **drops**, it can be a **shock** and make you feel even colder.

5 A car is easier to see than a person walking in the desert. You can also use the mirrors from your car to signal[2] to planes and other cars. You can use your car tires to make a fire. A fire is easy to see. It will help people find you, and it will keep you warm at night.

6 Try to drink some water at least once every hour. You need your water to last as long as possible. Drink only what you need. When you talk, you lose water from your body. Keep your mouth closed and do not talk.

7 If you eat, you will get thirsty and drink all of your water more quickly. You can eat a little, but only to stop you from feeling very hungry. Eat very small amounts of food, and eat very slowly. You can live three weeks with no food, but you can only live three days with no water.

8 It is very important to stay out of the sun during the day. Make a hole under your car and lie there. This will keep you cool and help you sleep. Find a warm place to sleep at night. A small place near a tree or a rock will be the warmest. But be **careful** before you **decide** where to sleep. Dangerous animals like snakes and scorpions also like to sleep in these places. Look carefully for animals before you lie down.

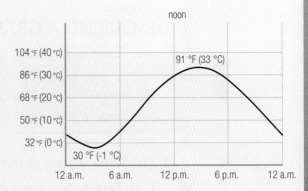

[1]**surviving** (v) staying alive in dangerous situations
[2]**signal** (v) make a sign or wave to get someone's attention

COLLOCATIONS WITH *TEMPERATURE*

PRISM Online Workbook

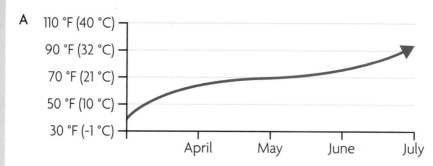

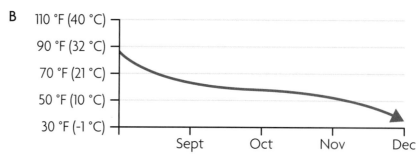

1 Look at the graphs. Circle the correct word to complete the sentences about the graphs.

1 In July, there are *high / low* temperatures.
2 In December, there are *high / low* temperatures.
3 The *maximum / minimum* temperature is 90 °F (32 °C) in July.
4 The *maximum / minimum* temperature is 34 °F (1°C) in December.

DESCRIBING A GRAPH

SKILLS

You can use certain words and phrases to talk about graphs. Use the verbs *rise, drop, fall,* and *reach* and the nouns *increase* and *decrease* to describe changes on a graph. *Increase* and *decrease* are also verbs.

PRISM Online Workbook

2 Match the sentences to the correct graph (A or B).

1 The graph shows an **increase** in temperature. _____
2 The graph shows a **decrease** in temperature. _____
3 The temperature **rises** to 90 °F (32 °C). _____
4 The temperature **drops** to 34 °F (1 °C). _____
5 The temperature **falls** to 34 °F (1 °C). _____
6 The temperature **reaches** 90 °F (32 °C). _____

3 Complete the statements with the bold words in Exercise 2.

1 Use _____ and _____ to talk about an increase in temperature.

2 Use _____ and _____ to talk about a decrease in temperature.

4 Look at the graphs. Circle the correct word to complete the sentences.

1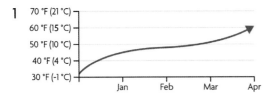

a The graph shows *an increase / a decrease* in temperature.

b In April, the temperature *reaches / falls to* 60° F (15 °C).

2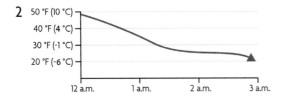

a The graph shows *an increase / a decrease* in temperature.

b At three o'clock, the temperature *drops / rises* to about 23 °F (-5 °C).

3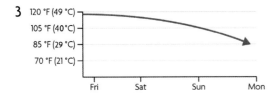

a The graph shows *an increase / a decrease* in temperature.

b On Monday, the temperature *reaches / falls to* 86 °F (30 °C).

4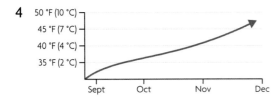

a The graph shows *an increase / a decrease* in temperature.

b In December, the temperature *rises / falls* to 45 °F (7 °C).

WRITING

CRITICAL THINKING

At the end of this unit, you will write a paragraph describing data from graphs. Look at this unit's Writing Task below.

▶ Describe the weather in a country or region.

SKILLS

Analyze a graph

You can use graphs to show numbers or data. When you look at a graph, you can see the most interesting information quickly and easily. When you write about graphs, choose the most interesting information to write about. To do this, look at the highest and lowest numbers.

UNDERSTAND

1 Look back at the graph in Reading 2 and answer the questions.

   1 What do the numbers on the left side of the graph show?
   2 What do the numbers at the bottom of the graph show?
   3 What does the highest point in the graph show?
   4 What does the lowest point in the graph show?

ANALYZE

2 Look at the graphs. What kind of information does each one show?

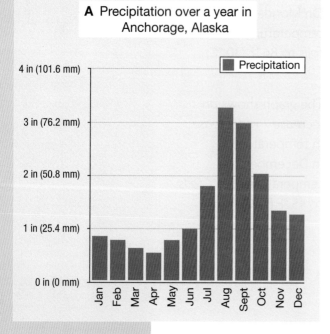

A Precipitation over a year in Anchorage, Alaska

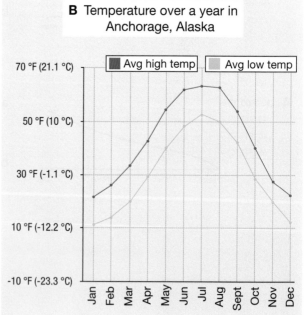

B Temperature over a year in Anchorage, Alaska

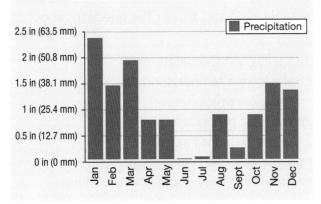

C Precipitation over a year in Amman, Jordan

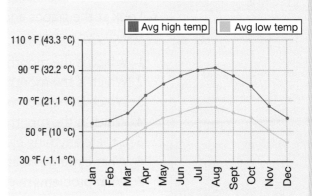

D Temperature over a year in Amman, Jordan

3 Circle the correct words to complete the sentences.

1 Graph A shows *temperature in Fahrenheit and Celsius / precipitation in inches and millimeters / the number of hurricanes.*

2 Graph B shows *temperature in Fahrenheit and Celsius / average hours of daylight / precipitation in inches.*

3 Graph C shows data for *Amman / Anchorage.*

4 Graph D shows *average temperatures / precipitation.*

5 Graphs A and C are *line graphs / bar graphs.*

6 Graphs B and D are *line graphs / bar graphs.*

4 Complete the table using the information from the graphs in Exercise 2.

Anchorage, Alaska

Months	Jan	Feb	Mar	Apr	May	Jun	Jul	Aug	Sept	Oct	Nov	Dec
Precipitation												
Average high temperature												
Average low temperature												

Amman, Jordan

Months	Jan	Feb	Mar	Apr	May	Jun	Jul	Aug	Sept	Oct	Nov	Dec
Precipitation												
Average high temperature												
Average low temperature												

5 Now choose one city that you will describe in your Writing Task at the end of this unit: Anchorage, Alaska or Amman, Jordan.

6 Look at the graphs and the table again and answer the questions about the city you chose.

1 Which is the month with the highest temperature?
2 Which is the month with the lowest temperature?
3 Which is the month with the most precipitation?
4 Which is the month with the least precipitation?
5 Is there anything else in the graph that is interesting?
6 What extreme weather do you think this place might have?
7 What problems might this cause for the people who live there?

GRAMMAR FOR WRITING

COMPARATIVE AND SUPERLATIVE ADJECTIVES

Comparative adjectives

Use a *comparative adjective* + *than* to show how two people, things, or ideas are different.

The Sahara Desert is **hotter than** Cairo.

For one-syllable adjectives, add -*er*.

warm → **warmer**

For one-syllable adjectives that end in one vowel and one consonant, double the consonant and add -*er*. Do not double the consonant *w*.

wet → **wetter**   low → **lower**

Remove the -*y* and add -*ier* to two-syllable adjectives ending in -*y*.

rainy → **rainier**   early → **earlier**   NOTE: dry → **drier**

Use *more* before almost all adjectives with two or more syllables. *Less* is the opposite of *more*.

beautiful → **more beautiful / less beautiful**

Some comparative adjectives are irregular.

good → **better**   bad → **worse**

Use *as* + *adjective* + *as* to say that two ideas are similar or the same. *Not as ... as* means "less than."

Cairo is **as hot as** Dubai.   Montreal is **not as hot as** Miami.

Superlative adjectives

Use *the + superlative adjective* to compare one person, thing, or idea to others. They mean "more / less than all of the others."

The Sahara Desert is **the hottest** place in Egypt.

Add *the … -est* to one-syllable adjectives.

cool → **the coolest**   cold → **the coldest**

For one-syllable adjectives that end in one vowel and one consonant, double the consonant and add *-est*. Do not double the consonant *w*.

hot → **the hottest**   low → **the lowest**

Remove the *-y* and add *-iest* to two-syllable adjectives ending in *-y*.

hungry → **the hungriest**   early → **the earliest**

Use *the most* before almost all adjectives with two or more syllables. Try to memorize the exceptions.

dangerous → **the most dangerous**

✗ the ~~most~~ hungriest

Some superlative adjectives are irregular.

good → **the best**   bad → **the worst**

1 Complete the table with the correct form of the adjective.

adjective	comparative	superlative
cold		
low		
extreme		
dry		
big		
easy		

2 Look at the fact files for Cuba and Iceland. Complete the sentences using the word in parentheses to make a comparative or superlative adjective.

🄵 CUBA

- Maximum temperature: 90 °F (32 °C)
- Minimum temperature: 64 °F (18 °C)
- Average rainfall: 6.9 in (173 mm)
- Average sunshine: 7.5 hours a day

🄵 ICELAND

- Maximum temperature: 57 °F (14 °C)
- Minimum temperature: 28 °F (-2 °C)
- Average rainfall: 3.8 in (94 mm)
- Average sunshine: 3.4 hours a day

1 Cuba has a _____ maximum temperature than Iceland. (high)
2 Iceland is _____ than Cuba. (cold)
3 Iceland has the _____ temperature. (low)
4 Cuba is _____ than Iceland. (wet)
5 Iceland is _____ than Cuba. (dry)
6 Cuba is the _____ country. (rainy)
7 Iceland is not as _____ as Cuba. (sunny)

ACADEMIC WRITING SKILLS

SUPPORTING SENTENCES

The *supporting sentences* in a paragraph give more information about the topic sentence. When writing about graphs, numbers (or *data*) are used to support main ideas.

Thunderstorms are common all over the world. **Weather experts estimate that there are 16 million thunderstorms around the world every year.**

1 In the pairs of sentences, underline the main idea. Circle the data.

1 The hottest time is between 2 p.m. and 4 p.m. Temperatures rise to 91 °F (33 °C).

2 The coldest time is at 4 a.m. Temperatures fall to 30 °F (-1 °C).

2 Match the sentence halves to complete the statements.

1 The main idea   a describes a general feature or trend from the graph.
2 The data   b is a number from the graph to illustrate the trend.

3 Match the main ideas to the data.

Main Ideas	Data
1 New York is as rainy as Houston.	**a** There are 8.7 hours of sunshine in July and 8 hours of sunshine in August.
2 The hottest month is March.	
3 July is sunnier than August.	**b** Temperatures reach 99 °F (37 °C).
4 The coldest month is December.	**c** Both cities have an average rainfall of 50 in (1,270 mm).
	d Temperatures fall to 19 °F (-7 °C).

4 Read the topic sentence. Then check all the supporting sentences that belong in the paragraph.

Topic sentence: The weather in Costa Rica changes in different regions.

a The rainiest area in the country is the northeast mountain region, which receives 141 in (3,580 mm) of rain each year. ☐

b The Central Valley, where the capital city of San Jose is located, has the mildest temperature year round. ☐

c In Costa Rica, the rainy season lasts from May to November. ☐

d At the beach, the temperature can rise to as high as 92 °F (33 °C). ☐

e In the rainforest, there are thousands of different types of animals to see. ☐

f On the highest mountain, called Cerro Chirripó, it can drop to below-freezing temperatures at night. ☐

GIVING EXAMPLES

SKILLS

Like, such as, and *for example*

In a supporting sentence, writers often give examples to support the main idea. Use *like, such as,* and *for example* to give an example or a list of examples.

Stay warm by wearing the right clothes, **like** a hat and a sweater.
Hurricanes are usually given names, **such as** Hurricane Sandy.
There are a lot of fun activities to do in the winter, **for example,** skiing and ice skating.

Use a comma before *like* and *such as*. Use a comma before and after *for example*.

5 Rewrite the sentences. Put the words in parentheses in the correct place and use *like*, *such as*, or *for example*. More than one answer is possible.

1 Wildfires have many different causes. (lightning)
   <u>Wildfires have many different causes, like lightning.</u>

2 It is too hot to snow in some U.S. cities. (Las Vegas, Miami)
   _____

3 There are a lot of tornadoes in certain states. (Oklahoma, Texas)
   _____

4 When you go camping, bring important items. (water, sunscreen)
   _____

WRITING TASK

Describe the weather in a country or region.

PLAN

1 Look back at the graphs and table for the city you chose in Critical Thinking. Write a topic sentence to describe the data in each table.

_____

_____

2 Choose the two most interesting facts about temperature. Write a sentence about each fact. Use data to support the statements.

_____

_____

3 Choose the two most interesting facts about precipitation. Write a sentence about each fact. Use data to support the statements.

_____

_____

4 Refer to the Task Checklist on page 99 as you prepare your paragraph.

WRITE A FIRST DRAFT

5 Write a first draft of your paragraph.

REVISE

6 Use the Task Checklist to review your paragraph for content and structure.

TASK CHECKLIST	✔
Did you write a topic sentence and supporting sentences?	
Did you give examples with *like*, *such as*, and *for example*?	
Did you write about precipitation and temperature?	
Did you compare data from the graphs?	
Have you used data from the graphs to support the main ideas?	

7 Make any necessary changes to your paragraph.

EDIT

8 Use the Language Checklist to edit your paragraph for language errors.

LANGUAGE CHECKLIST	✔
Did you use the correct collocations with *temperature*?	
Did you use the correct vocabulary to describe the graphs?	
Did you use comparative and superlative adjectives correctly?	

9 Make any necessary changes to your paragraph.

SEEING A DOCTOR

Staying healthy is important to all of us. It's good to find a doctor before you get sick. It's also good to know about the health care system.

PREPARING TO READ

1 Work with a partner. Discuss the questions.

1 What are common reasons people go to a doctor?
2 Where do people go when they need to see a doctor? Where do they go in an emergency?
3 How do people make a doctor's appointment?

WHILE READING

2 Read the brochure from the Health Center. Complete the sentences with the correct word or phrase.

1 The _____ is only for people who are very sick or injured.
2 A student should bring a _____ and an _____ to a doctor's appointment.
3 If a student doesn't know how to describe his or her symptoms well, he or she should ask for a _____ .
4 Students should visit the _____ if they are going to travel to a foreign country.

PRACTICE

3 Imagine that you don't feel well and you are at the health center. Answer the questions with your own information.

- What is the reason for today's visit?
- When did this problem begin?
- Describe your symptoms.
- What medications do you take?
- Do you have any allergies?
- Do you smoke? If yes, how much?
- Have you had any serious injuries or illnesses in the past year?
- Do you have any other health issues you want to discuss?

River College Health Center
Medical Care for All Students
Open 6 a.m.–6 p.m. Monday–Friday

OUR CLINICS
+ General Medicine Clinic
+ Women's Clinic
+ Travel Clinic
+ Emergency Room (open 24/7, for serious illness or injury only)

OUR SERVICES
+ Pharmacy services
+ After-hours nurse services by phone
+ Translators for most languages

What to bring
+ a photo ID
+ your insurance card

AT THE DOCTOR'S OFFICE
Common reasons to see a doctor
+ fever
+ coughing more than 2 weeks
+ sore throat
+ depression
+ feeling tired for several weeks
+ stomach hurts for a week
+ back pain
+ flu shot
+ quitting smoking

REAL-WORLD APPLICATION

4 Work in small groups.

1 Visit the health center or clinic on or near your campus, or visit the clinic website.
2 Find out this information:
   • When are they open?
   • What services do they provide?
   • How does someone make an appointment?
   • Do they have an emergency clinic?
3 With your group, make a brochure about the clinic.
4 Share your brochure with your class.

ACTIVATE YOUR KNOWLEDGE

Discuss the questions with a partner.

1 Look at the photo. What sport do you see?
2 Do you play any sports? Why or why not?
3 Do you like watching sports? If so, which sports do you enjoy watching?
4 Do you have a favorite team or player?
5 Why do you think people like watching sports?

WATCH AND LISTEN

PREPARING TO WATCH

ACTIVATING YOUR
KNOWLEDGE

1 Work with a partner and answer the questions.

1 What are some mountain sports?
2 What sports include racing?
3 What sports are in the Winter Olympics?

PREDICTING CONTENT
USING VISUALS

2 You are going to watch a video about a winter sport. Look at the pictures from the video. What are the people doing? Discuss your answers with your partner.

GLOSSARY

slalom (n) a race, especially down a mountain on skis, in which the competitors follow a path that curves around a series of poles

smooth (adj) having a surface with no holes or lumps in it; glass is usually smooth

wax (n) a solid substance that becomes soft when warm and melts easily, often used to make candles

---

WHILE WATCHING

UNDERSTANDING
DETAILS

3 ▶ Watch the video. Complete each sentence with a word from the box. You will use five of the seven words.

> best   blue   dangerous   green
> popular   rich   well-known

1 Courchevel is a very _____ place for skiing.
2 Some of the world's _____ skiers go to Courchevel.
3 Courchevel 1850 is the highest and most _____ village.
4 Many _____ and famous people like to ski here.
5 Slalom skiers race down the mountain between _____ and red flags.

4 ▶ Watch again. Correct the mistakes in the student's notes.

> **1** Emma is a British Olympic swimmer.
>
> **2** She was in the Olympics two times.
>
> **3** Dallas Campbell is an Olympic skier.
>
> **4** Emma and Dallas are racing up the mountain.
>
> **5** The difference between 1st and 10th place is less than one minute.
>
> **6** Wax makes skis go slow.

5 ▶ Watch again. How do they prepare the skis? Put the steps in the order you hear them (1–4). Compare your answers with a partner.

UNDERSTANDING MAIN IDEAS

  a Then they make the skis smooth again. _____
  b Next, they fill the holes with wax. _____
  c The skis are now ready. _____
  d First, they grind the bottom of the skis. _____

6 Work with a partner. What are two other reasons people might go to Courchevel?

MAKING INFERENCES

  a _____   **b** _____

DISCUSSION

7 Work with a partner. Discuss the questions.

  1 Do you think skiing is easy? Is it dangerous? Explain your answers.
  2 What are some racing sports in your country?
  3 Have you ever been in a race? If so, describe the race and the experience.

8 Work in small groups. You need skis, poles, glasses or goggles, boots, and snow for skiing. Look at the sports in the box, and decide what things you need for them.

> baseball   cycling   fishing   golf
> ice hockey   soccer   swimming   tennis

READING

PREPARING TO READ

UNDERSTANDING KEY VOCABULARY

1 Read the definitions. Complete the sentences with the correct form of the words in bold.

> **ancient** (adj) from a long time ago; very old
> **compete** (v) to take part in a race or competition; to try to be more successful than someone else
> **competition** (n) an organized event in which people try to win a prize by being the best
> **strange** (adj) not familiar; difficult to understand; different
> **swimming** (n) a sport where people move through water by moving their body
> **take place** (phr v) to happen
> **throw** (v) to send something through the air, pushing it out of your hand

1 The baseball game will _____ tomorrow at 2 p.m. in the park.
2 Thousands of people from all over the world _____ the New York City Marathon every year. The fastest runners can win a lot of money.
3 Boxing is a(n) _____ sport; it was popular in Rome thousands of years ago.
4 The first cricket game I ever saw was _____ because I didn't understand the rules. Once I learned more about the sport, I became a big fan.
5 In baseball, players must be able to _____ the ball a long distance directly to another player.
6 The best tennis players were selected from each high school in the city. They will play in a(n) _____ to see who is the best tennis player in the city.
7 Because Elsa grew up near the ocean, her favorite sport was _____ . Her parents said she was just like a fish.

Scanning to predict content

Before reading a text, skilled readers often scan for *key words*. Key words are usually nouns, verbs, and adjectives. The key words tell the reader what the text is going to be about.

2 Look at the underlined words in paragraph 1 of the text on page 108. Answer the questions.

1 What is the main topic of the text?
   a unusual competitions
   b unusual sports
   c popular sports
2 Where do the events in the text happen?
   a in one country
   b around the world
   c in a city
3 Look at the underlined words again. What types of words are they? More than one answer is possible.
   a verbs
   b adjectives
   c articles
   d nouns
   e prepositions

3 Read the text and check your answers to Exercise 2.

Five Unusual Sports
The Most Unusual Sports from Around the World

1 Every <u>country</u> has a national <u>sport</u>, and most popular <u>sports</u> are now played across the <u>world</u>. Most people have heard of <u>sports</u> like football, basketball, baseball, and soccer. However, in most <u>countries</u>, people also play <u>unusual sports</u> with **strange** and interesting rules. Here are our top five <u>unusual sports</u> from around the world.

2 _____

People go **swimming** in the Atlantic Ocean in the winter. They go swimming at the beach on Coney Island in New York City every Sunday from October to April and also on New Year's Day. The water temperature can drop to as low as 32 °F (0 °C). Sometimes there is snow and cold wind, too. People believe that swimming in the cold water is good for their health. The club started in 1903.

3 _____

Every year in Singapore, thousands of people come to watch the dragon boat race. A dragon boat is a traditional Chinese boat with a painted dragon's head on one end. There are 22 people in each boat, and they race in the water. Dragon boat racing is also popular in China, Malaysia, and Indonesia.

4 _____

In this sport, people **compete** by **throwing** a large piece of wood called a "caber" as far as they can. The caber toss is an **ancient** Scottish sport. The caber has no official size or shape, but it is usually the size of a small tree.

5 _____

Students in Indonesia play this game to welcome the month of Ramadan. It is similar to soccer. The ball is made from coconut shells. Before starting the game, players pour salt on themselves and then light the ball on fire. The ball is on fire throughout the game, and the players play with their bare[1] feet.

6 _____

In Turkey, camel wrestling[2] is a very old sport. The largest camel wrestling **competition takes place** in Ephesus every year, and thousands of people come to watch. In the sport, two male camels wrestle each other. Sometimes the camels do not want to fight, and they run through the crowds, which can be dangerous.

[1]**bare** (adj) without shoes

[2]**wrestling** (n) a sport in which two people (or, in this case, animals) fight and try to push each other to the ground

WHILE READING

4 Read the titles below. Write the titles above each paragraph in the text.

    a Fireball Soccer
    b Dragon Boat Racing
    c Camel Wrestling
    d Caber Toss
    e Coney Island Polar Bear Plunge

READING FOR
MAIN IDEAS

5 Write the names of the countries where each sport is popular.

    1 Fireball soccer _____
    2 Dragon boat race _____
    3 Camel wrestling _____
    4 Caber toss _____
    5 Coney Island Polar Bear Plunge _____

6 Read the text again and look at the sentences. There is one mistake in each sentence. Correct the false information.

READING FOR DETAILS

    1 The Coney Island Polar Bear Plunge takes place every Sunday from October to April and on Christmas Day.

    _____

    2 The Coney Island Polar Bear Plunge began in 2003.

    _____

    3 A dragon boat has a dragon's tail painted on it.

    _____

    4 There are 25 people in each dragon boat team.

    _____

    5 A caber is a large piece of metal.

    _____

    6 A caber is usually the size of a large tree.

    _____

    7 In fireball soccer, the ball is made from plastic.

    _____

    8 The ball is on fire only at the beginning of a game of fireball soccer.

    _____

    9 The Ephesus camel wrestling competition happens twice a year.

    _____

    10 In camel wrestling, two female camels fight each other.

    _____

READING BETWEEN THE LINES

7 Answer the questions.

1 What kind of person is this text for?
   a someone who is interested in different sports
   b someone who wants to learn how to play a new sport
2 Where do you think you might see this text?
   a in a newspaper or magazine
   b on a website
3 What do you think the text is?
   a an advertisement
   b an article

DISCUSSION

8 Discuss the questions with a partner.

1 What are the advantages of playing sports?
2 Why do countries spend large amounts of money to organize sporting events like the Olympic Games?

READING 2

PREPARING TO READ

1 Read the sentences and choose the best definition for the words in bold.

1 In January 2015, the Hong Kong Marathon had over 73,000 **participants**.
   a people who take part in an activity
   b people who organize an activity
2 The golf **course** was so big that the players drove golf carts to get from hole to hole.
   a an area used for sporting events, such as racing or playing golf
   b an area where players get together after they finish a sport
3 It takes about six hours to **climb** Mount Fuji in Japan. Many people try to reach the top just before the sun rises.
   a wait for something to start
   b go up something or onto the top of something
4 There was an **accident** during the car race yesterday. One car hit another, and they both rolled over. Luckily, neither driver was hurt.
   a something bad that happens that is not intended and that causes injury or damage
   b something that someone does in order to hurt another person

5 In order to stay **in shape**, you should eat foods that are good for you, exercise, and stay active.
  a interesting because you like different things
  b in good health; strong

6 One of the most **challenging** games is table tennis, which is also called Ping-Pong. Players must be strong, quick, and able to focus on the ball for long periods of time.
  a easy to learn
  b difficult in a way that tests your ability

2 Before you read, look at the text on page 112. What type of text is it?

3 Look at the photos and read the title of the text. What do you think the topic of the text will be?

4 Read the text on page 112 and check your answers to Exercises 2 and 3.

PREVIEWING

WHILE READING

5 Read the text again and circle the correct words to complete the sentences.

1 Tough Guy is a very *easy / difficult* competition.
2 The event takes place when it is very *hot / cold*.
3 People from many different *countries / cities* take part.
4 Every year, people *get hurt / leave early*.
5 Participants have to be very *smart / strong* to do the event.
6 The competition is *different / the same* every year.

READING FOR MAIN IDEAS

6 Look at the diagram of the course on page 112. Match the different parts of the competition to the facts from the final paragraph of the text.

1 mud run
2 nets
3 high dive and swim
4 field of fire
5 water tunnel
6 nettles

a Participants must crawl through something wet.
b The runners run and jump over small bonfires.
c The runners run 1.2 miles (2 kilometers) through a field of plants that may hurt them.
d Participants run for 0.6 miles (1 kilometer) along a road that is wet and dirty.
e The runners jump off a platform into a lake and swim for 0.6 miles (1 kilometer).
f They crawl low on the ground.

TOUGH¹ GUY:
A Race to the Limit

1 What is Tough Guy?

Every January, more than 3,000 people take part in one of the most difficult races on Earth: the Tough Guy competition in the U.K. **Participants** run, swim, and **climb** across the 9-mile (15-kilometer) **course**. But this is no normal race. These runners have to crawl through tunnels, run across a field of nettles, and jump over fire. What's more, the competition takes place in January, so temperatures are freezing—sometimes as low as 21 °F (-6 °C). People travel from all over the world to take part, with participants from the U.S., Australia, and China.

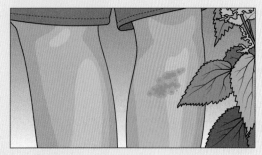

2 Why do people take part?

The competition is very dangerous and every year there are **accidents**. Injuries like broken bones and cuts are common. The race is very hard: one-third of participants do not finish it. Runners have to be healthy and **in shape**. Most people train all year to prepare for the event. It is also the first race like it in the world. Many people take part in the competition because it is so famous. Every year, the organizers change the event and add new things. This means that the competition stays exciting and **challenging**, so people go back year after year.

3 The course

The diagram shows an example of the Tough Guy course. First, participants run for 0.6 miles (1 kilometer) along a muddy road. Next, they crawl under low nets on the ground. After the nets, the runners jump off a high platform into a lake and swim for another 0.6 miles (1 kilometer). Then they reach the field of fire. Here the runners run across a field and jump over small bonfires. Next, participants must crawl through a long tunnel. The tunnel is partly underwater. Finally, the runners run 1.2 miles (2 kilometers) through nettles before they reach the finish line.

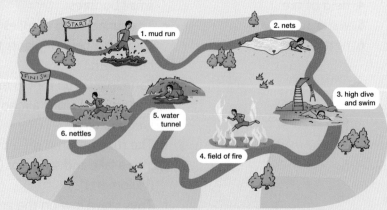

¹**tough** (adj) physically strong and not afraid

7 Answer the questions.

1 Where does the Tough Guy competition take place?

_____

2 When does the Tough Guy competition take place?

_____

3 How long is the course? _____

4 How long do people train for the competition? _____

5 Why do people go back to the competition every year?

_____

8 Match the verbs to the correct phrases. Each verb has two answers.

1 crawl
2 run
3 jump

a over small bonfires
b across a field of nettles
c under low nets
d across a field of fire
e through tunnels
f off a high platform

READING BETWEEN THE LINES

9 Circle the correct answer.

1 The text says that participants have to *run through nettles*. Look at the images and the text. What is a nettle?
   a a plant
   b an animal

2 Why do you think running through nettles is difficult?
   a because nettles hurt you
   b because nettles smell horrible

DISCUSSION

10 Discuss the questions with a partner.

1 Do you know any events like the Tough Guy competition?
2 Why do people stay in shape in their free time?
3 Should people be allowed to do dangerous sports like horse riding and skiing?

11 Work with a partner. Use ideas from Reading 1 and Reading 2 to answer the questions.

1 What are three questions you would like to ask someone who took part in one of the sports from Reading 1 or Reading 2?
2 Which sport from Reading 1 or Reading 2 would be the most popular in your country? Why? Which one would be the least popular? Why?

⊙ LANGUAGE DEVELOPMENT

PREPOSITIONS OF MOVEMENT

Prepositions of movement describe where someone or something is going. Use prepositions of movement to give directions.

Walk **past** the school and **across** the road.

PRISM Online Workbook

1 Match the descriptions to the pictures.

1 past the building

2 through the tunnel

3 across the lake

4 around the track

5 along the road

6 over the bridge

7 under the bridge

2 Look at the map. Use the prepositions from Exercise 1 to complete the paragraph. You may need to use some prepositions more than once.

It is easy to get to my house. First, walk (1)_____ Main Street. Go (2)_____ the bank and (3)_____ the bridge. Then walk (4)_____ the park and (5)_____ the next bridge. Go (6)_____ the tunnel—watch out for cars—and walk (7)_____ the road. Walk (8)_____ the lake. My house is at the end of the road.

WRITING

CRITICAL THINKING

At the end of this unit, you will write a process paragraph. Look at this unit's Writing Task below.

> Describe the Sydney Triathlon.

Analyzing a diagram

In academic writing, you often have to write about diagrams. It is important to analyze the information in the diagram carefully before you write. Sometimes you will need to understand the order of the events in the diagram and the effect that different events have on each other.

1 Look at the diagram of the triathlon course in Sydney. Label the diagram with the words from the box. Use the key to help you.

ANALYZE ▲

| central library | bridge | tunnel |
| bike route | running route | swim route |

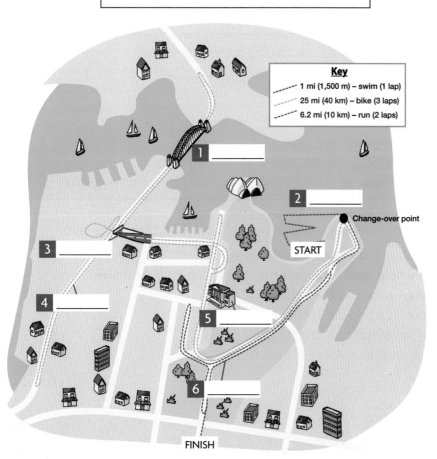

Key
— 1 mi (1,500 m) – swim (1 lap)
— 25 mi (40 km) – bike (3 laps)
— 6.2 mi (10 km) – run (2 laps)

1 _____

2 _____

● Change-over point

3 _____

4 _____

5 _____

6 _____

START

FINISH

2 Look at the diagram again and answer the questions.

1 How far do the participants have to run?

_____

2 How far do the participants have to swim?

_____

3 How far do the participants have to ride a bike?

_____

◢ APPLY

3 Look at the diagram again. What do the competitors in the triathlon have to do? Use prepositions to complete the phrases.

a ride a bike _____ the bridge

b ride a bike _____ the tunnel

c run _____ the road

d swim _____ the lake 1

e ride a bike _____ the central library

4 Number the parts of the race in Exercise 3 to show the correct order of the triathlon.

GRAMMAR FOR WRITING

SUBJECT AND VERB AGREEMENT

LANGUAGE

In a sentence, the form of the verb has to match the subject.

Use the *singular* form of the verb with singular subjects.
The race **begins** at 3 p.m.
The winner of last year's race **is** at the starting line.

Use the *plural* form of the verb with plural subjects.
The soccer players **play** three times a week.
Soccer and tennis **are** popular sports.

PRISM Online Workbook

1 Look at the sentences. Underline the subject and circle the verb.

1 The boys and girls play sports every day.

2 The whole family watches the World Cup finals at home.

3 Aisha runs across the field.

4 Soccer is a popular sport in Europe.

5 The racers run over the bridge.

6 Hanh and I love Formula One racing.

2 Circle the correct form of the verb in the sentences.

1 Julia *is / are* a tennis player.
2 The coach *swim / swims* every day.
3 The cycling team *rides / ride* over the bridge.
4 The fastest runner *win / wins* the trophy.
5 Oleg and I *practice / practices* hockey after school.
6 Skiing *are / is* a winter sport.

3 Complete the sentences with the correct form of the verb in parentheses.

1 I _____ (try) to practice every day.
2 The team captain _____ (carry) the trophy.
3 Dragon boat racing _____ (be) an unusual sport.
4 My friends and I _____ (watch) sports on TV.
5 Soccer players often _____ (miss) penalty goals.
6 He _____ (want) to be a Formula One driver.
7 The teams and the referee _____ (run) onto the field.
8 Football and basketball _____ (be) popular sports in the U.S.
9 The players _____ (catch) the ball.

ACADEMIC WRITING SKILLS

ORDERING EVENTS IN A PROCESS

When writing about a process, academic writers usually write about events in the order that they happen. *Transition words* are used to organize ideas and show the order in writing.

Use the transition words *first*, *second*, *third*, and *finally* to show the order in which events happen in a process. You can also use *next*, *then*, and *after that* to show order.

First, the participants run 6.2 miles (10 kilometers). **Second**, they swim across the river.

Participants run 6.2 miles (10 kilometers). **Then**, they swim across the river.

Use these transition words at the beginning of a sentence, followed by a comma.

1 Match the sentences to the pictures.

1 The weightlifter lifts the weight onto his shoulders. _____
2 The weightlifter drops the weight to the ground. _____
3 The weightlifter lifts the weight above his head. _____
4 The weightlifter holds the weight above his head for as long as he can. _____

a

b

c

d

2 Rewrite the sentences in Exercise 1 in the correct order using *first*, *second*, *third*, and *finally*.

1 _____

2 _____

3 _____

4 _____

3 Rewrite the paragraph with the words from the box to show the order of the events. Remember to use commas. More than one answer is possible.

| next   then   after that |

> The players walk onto the court. They pick up their rackets. One player hits the ball over the net. The other player hits the ball back.

_____

_____

_____

_____

4 Compare and discuss your answers with a partner.

REMOVING UNRELATED INFORMATION

When writing, it is important to write only about information that is related or useful to the topic. Before you write, decide what information is important and only write about information that is directly related to or useful for the question. After you finish, it is a good idea to check for any information that is not important and delete it.

5 Read the writing prompt and the student's paragraph. Cross out the information in the paragraph that is not important.

Write a process paragraph to describe how to do the high jump.

The high jump is an Olympic sport that is practiced in many countries. ~~Athletes competed in over 30 venues during the 2012 London Olympic Games~~. First, the high jumper runs toward the bar. It is important to run very fast. The high jump is the most popular sport in Russia. Second, the high jumper jumps. I was on the track-and-field team at school. The high jumper must jump from the right foot and keep their arms close to their sides. Next, the high jumper twists their body so that their back is to the bar. They must lift their head and feet and keep them high above the bar. The high jump is a really interesting sport. After that, the high jumper lands. They must be careful to land safely on the mat. Derek Drouin from Canada won the gold medal in the men's high jump at the 2016 Rio Olympic Games, and Ruth Beitia from Spain won the gold for the women's high jump. Finally, the high jumper stands up, takes a bow, and leaves the mat.

6 Compare and discuss your answers with a partner.

Describe the Sydney Triathlon.

PLAN

1 Use your notes from Critical Thinking to complete the paragraph planner. Write any general information in column A. Put the events in the Sydney Triathlon in the correct order in column B.

A	B
	1
	2
	3
	4
	5

2 Refer to the Task Checklist on page 121 as you prepare your paragraph.

WRITE A FIRST DRAFT

3 Start your paragraph by writing a topic sentence about the general information in the diagram.

4 Write supporting sentences about the events in the triathlon in the correct order and use transition words to show the time order.

REVISE

5 Use the Task Checklist to review your paragraph for content and structure.

TASK CHECKLIST	✔
Did you write about the general information and the events in the Sydney Triathlon?	
Did you put the events in the correct order?	
Did you use transition words to show the order of the events clearly?	
Did you avoid using unrelated information?	

6 Make any necessary changes to your paragraph.

EDIT

7 Use the Language Checklist to edit your paragraph for language errors.

LANGUAGE CHECKLIST	✔
Did you use the correct prepositions of movement?	
Did you use subject and verb agreement correctly?	

8 Make any necessary changes to your paragraph.

VIRTUAL COMMUNICATION

SKILLS

Classmates often work together on group projects or in study groups. Communicating well with classmates outside of class is important. Sometimes, students also need to communicate with professors outside of class.

PREPARING TO READ

1 Work with a partner. Discuss the questions.

1 If you have a group project, how do you communicate and share work with your group?

2 How often do you communicate with classmates in a group project? How quickly do you respond to your classmates?

WHILE READING

2 Read a student blog about communicating in group projects.

3 Write *T* (true), *F* (false), or *DNS* (does not say) next to the statements.

_____ 1 The author thinks the most important thing in a group project is replying quickly.

_____ 2 When you change a shared file, you should give it a new name.

_____ 3 The author prefers email when she does group projects.

_____ 4 You shouldn't be late for a conference call.

_____ 5 If you can't finish on time, you should tell your group.

_____ 6 It's important to respond within a week.

PRACTICE

4 Work with a partner. Read Erika's blog again. Write one more tip for a successful group project for each type of communication: email, file sharing, group text, and video hangout or conference call.

Email: _____

File sharing: _____

Group text: _____

Video hangout or conference call: _____

COMMUNICATION IN GROUP PROJECTS

by Erika Vikstrom

Communicating with your group in a group project is important, but what's the best way to do it?

Here are a few tips about communicating for a successful group project:

1 Respond to others quickly, in 1 or 2 days.
2 Stay on topic.
3 Be honest if your part is late, or if you are having trouble. Your team can help!
4 If you want feedback, tell your group what you want to know.
5 Answer the questions that your team members ask.
6 Be respectful of others. Say "please" and "thank you." Think before you respond.

Here are some tips for different types of communication:

Email

This is a good way to discuss the project details.

- When you reply, include the original message.
- Use Reply All so everyone gets to be part of the email.

File sharing

This is helpful for sharing your work.

- Check regularly for any changes or updates.
- If you make a change to a file, save the new file with a new name.

Group text

A group text is usually the fastest way to get information to all team members.

- Use texts for reminders or short messages.
- Don't send too many texts.

Video hangouts or conference calls

It's a good idea to have a few virtual meetings for everyone to discuss the project. Be on time, and be prepared.

The most important thing is that everyone does their part. Good luck with your group projects!

REAL-WORLD APPLICATION

5 Do a survey with your group. Ask three people these questions.

1 How often do you do a group project in class?
☐ weekly ☐ monthly ☐ never ☐ other: _____

2 How do you communicate with people in a group project?
☐ email ☐ text ☐ social media ☐ class website
☐ phone ☐ video chat ☐ other: _____
Which do you prefer?

3 What are some good rules for communicating during group projects?

6 Report the answers back to your class.

7 As a class, make a list of dos and don'ts for communicating with classmates in a group project.

LEARNING OBJECTIVES

Reading skills	Work out meaning from context; annotate a text
Grammar	The simple present and the simple past; time clauses with *when* to describe past events
Academic writing skill	Add details to main facts
Writing Task	Write a narrative paragraph
On Campus	Create checklists

ACTIVATE YOUR KNOWLEDGE

1 Discuss the questions with a partner.

a An *entrepreneur* is a person who starts a new business. Do you know the names of the famous entrepreneurs in the photos?

b Do you know the names of the companies they started?

c Do you know the names of any other famous entrepreneurs from your country?

2 Look at the words in the box. Which of these are important qualities for an entrepreneur to have?

> careful   smart   friendly   good with computers   polite
> good with money   happy   hardworking   kind   funny

3 Do you think you would be a good entrepreneur? Why or why not?

WATCH AND LISTEN

PREPARING TO WATCH

ACTIVATING YOUR KNOWLEDGE

1 Work with a partner and answer the questions.

1 Why do people shop online?
2 What do people usually buy online?
3 What was the last thing you bought online? What about in a store?

USING YOUR KNOWLEDGE

2 You are going to watch a video about the online store Amazon. Read the statements. Check (✔) the ones that you think are true.

1 ☐ There are millions of things to buy at Amazon.
2 ☐ A computer finds your things after you order them.
3 ☐ Amazon does not sell kitchen things.

> **GLOSSARY**
>
> **warehouse** (n) a large building for keeping things that are going to be sold
> **item** (n) a single thing in a set or on a list, such as a book or a toy
> **fulfillment** (n) the act of doing something that you promised to do
> **central** (adj) main or most important; organized and working from one main place
> **random** (adj) done or chosen without any plan or system

WHILE WATCHING

3 ▶ Watch the video. Check your answers in Exercise 2.

4 ▶ Watch again. Put a check (✔) next to the things you see.

UNDERSTANDING DETAILS

1 ☐ a shelf   6 ☐ a male worker
2 ☐ a yellow bin   7 ☐ a toy
3 ☐ a warehouse   8 ☐ a computer
4 ☐ a book   9 ☐ a box
5 ☐ a large cart   10 ☐ tape

5 ▶ Watch again. Complete the summary with numbers or words. Check your answers with a partner.

Amazon's first warehouse was in (1)_____ , Washington. It has more than (2)_____ million items for sale on its (3)_____ . Amazon has many (4)_____ warehouses around the world. They are called (5)_____ centers.

6 Write *T* (true) or *F* (false) next to the statements. Correct the false statements.

_____ 1 Amazon is the world's largest online store.

_____ 2 The first warehouse was a kitchen.

_____ 3 Only the workers know where everything is.

_____ 4 An Amazon worker finds your item before you pay for it.

_____ 5 Any item can be on any shelf in the warehouse.

7 Put the sentences in the order that they happen in the video (1–5). Compare your answers with a partner.

a The box leaves the warehouse. _____

b The computer tells the workers the correct size of the box. _____

c An Amazon worker finds your item. _____

d You order and pay for an item online. _____

e Your name and address go on the box. _____

8 Work with a partner. Why does the speaker in the video say that "an item's location is random so that workers don't take the wrong item"? Circle the best answer.

a The central computer always makes mistakes.

b The worker might choose the wrong item if two similar items were together.

c Amazon trusts its computers more than its workers.

DISCUSSION

9 Work with a partner. Discuss the questions. Explain your answers.

1. In the future, what jobs will computers do that people do today?

2 What jobs will humans always do?

3 What do you think is the future of physical stores?

4 Which items are better to buy at a store than online?

> books   clothes   eyeglasses   food   furniture
> jewelry   music   plants   tickets   vitamins

READING

PREPARING TO READ

UNDERSTANDING KEY VOCABULARY

1 Read the sentences and choose the best definition for the words in bold.

1 Marta likes to **organize** her schedule at work. She puts her meetings and tasks in a calendar so that she gets everything done on time.
   a plan or arrange carefully
   b lose easily

2 Ken found a job he wants to do. He wants to **apply** for it this week and hopes to get the job.
   a share thoughts and ideas
   b ask officially for something, often by writing

3 Emre just shared the **results** of the company survey. He says that a lot of people are happy with the company's work.
   a information that you find out from something, such as an exam, a scientific experiment, or a medical test
   b questions people ask to find out more information

4 Grace is trying to decide on an **occupation**. She wants to be either a doctor or an engineer.
   a homework   b a job or career

5 My **colleague** and I are writing a new computer program. We work late every night because our boss wants us to finish it quickly.
   a someone that you live next to   b someone that you work with

6 The new store on Main Street is doing really well. A lot of **customers** go there and buy things.
   a people who buy things from a store or business
   b people who sell things at a store or business

SCANNING TO PREDICT CONTENT

2 Before you read, look at the text on page 129 quickly. Circle the answers.

1 What kind of text is it?
   a an encyclopedia entry
   b an online quiz
   c a newspaper article

2 Which question is the best description of the topic?
   a What would be your perfect job?
   b Could you start your own company?
   c What makes a good businessperson?

3 Read the text and check your answers.

Are You Ready for the World of Work?

Do you know what kind of job you want? Before you **apply** for a job, think about the different types of jobs that people do. There are four main types of jobs:

1 jobs with people
2 jobs with information
3 jobs with things
4 jobs with ideas

What kind of work would be best for you? Take our quiz and find out about the kind of work you would enjoy. For each question, choose the best answer for you: **a**, **b**, **c**, or **d**.

Check your results and read the advice to find occupations you would like.

1 **What do you like to do in the evenings?**
- ○ a meet friends or go to a party
- ○ b stay at home and surf the Internet
- ○ c play sports or practice a hobby like a musical instrument or photography
- ○ d go to the movies

2 **Which sections of the newspaper do you look at first?**
- ○ a advice column or letters to the editor
- ○ b news
- ○ c sports
- ○ d TV, music, books, and art

3 **What do you like to do at a party?**
- ○ a meet new people
- ○ b discuss the latest news
- ○ c help with the food and drinks
- ○ d sing songs and tell jokes

4 **What do you prefer to do on a day off?**
- ○ a have coffee with friends
- ○ b **organize** your books and cabinets
- ○ c work in the garden or clean your house
- ○ d write poetry, make music, or draw pictures

Mostly "a" answers:
You are friendly, kind, and interested in other people. You would enjoy a job working with children, **customers** in a store, or on a team with **colleagues**. Possible jobs are: teacher, waiter, police officer.

Mostly "b" answers:
You are neat, good at planning, and you like learning new things. You would enjoy a job working with information. Possible jobs are: college professor, computer programmer, librarian.

Mostly "c" answers:
You are practical, good at sports, and you like working with your hands. You would enjoy a job working with things. Possible jobs are: construction worker, engineer, farmer.

Mostly "d" answers:
You are creative, good at music and art, and you like books. You would enjoy a job working with ideas. Possible jobs are: artist, writer, singer.

WHILE READING

4 Read the quiz again. Correct the mistakes in the paragraph using words from the quiz.

> There are three main kinds of work – work with animals, work with information, work with machines, and work with ideas. The quiz helps you to find out about the kind of people you might like. After the quiz, read the advice to find universities you may like.

5 Do the quiz in the text. Circle your answers and count the letters you chose. Read the advice about jobs for you.

6 Do you agree or disagree with the advice?

READING BETWEEN THE LINES

Working out meaning from context

Readers often see words in a text that they do not know. However, it is often possible to understand the meaning of new words in a text from the context (the topic and the other words in the text).

7 Find the words from the box in the quiz and underline them.

> hobby   neat   advice   sections

8 Read the text around the underlined words in the quiz. Circle the best definition for each word.

  1 advice (n)
    a an opinion that someone offers you about what you should do
    b instructions to tell someone exactly what to do
  2 hobby (n)
    a an activity you do for fun
    b a job
  3 section (n)
    a a type of reading material
    b one of the parts that something is divided into
  4 neat (adj)
    a arranged well, with everything in its place
    b not organized

9 Who would be interested in the quiz? Circle the correct answer. More than one answer is possible.

    a a new worker in a company
    b a new college graduate
    c a high school student

IDENTIFYING AUDIENCE

DISCUSSION

10 Discuss the questions with a partner.

    1 What would be your perfect job?
    2 What type of job would you hate?

READING 2

PREPARING TO READ

1 Read the sentences and write the words in bold next to the definitions.

    1 I want to be a doctor. I can reach my **goal** by studying hard.
    2 The company **introduced** a new tablet, and it sold out in one day.
    3 A lot of new jobs were created by the automobile factory. They **employ** more than 300 people in the community.
    4 Akiko shares an **office** with her coworker. It is small, and they don't have a lot of space for their desks and files.
    5 Manuel is my business **partner**. We opened a restaurant together.
    6 I'm going to **set up** a new business in my garage next year.
    7 The company needs to **advertise** its new smartphone on TV and on the Internet so that more people know about it and want to buy it.
    8 My mother **runs** her own business.

UNDERSTANDING KEY VOCABULARY

PRISM Online Workbook

    a _____ (phr v) to create or establish (something) for a particular purpose
    b _____ (n) a place in a building where people work
    c _____ (v) to manage or operate something
    d _____ (n) someone who runs or owns a business with another person
    e _____ (n) something you want to do successfully in the future
    f _____ (v) to pay someone to work or do a job for you
    g _____ (v) to make something available to buy or use for the first time
    h _____ (v) to tell people about a product or service, for example in newspapers or on television, in order to persuade them to buy it

2 Look at the article on page 133 and notice the words in bold from Exercise 1. Read the title. What do you think the article is about?

WHILE READING

SKILLS

Annotating a text

Effective readers take notes and *annotate* as they read. When you annotate, you write notes on the same page as the text. Annotating will help you to remember key information. For example, you can underline, circle, or highlight important words, numbers, and ideas. You can write main ideas and definitions of words in the margin. Annotating a text can also help you to study for tests or write about a text. For example:

> *all the people able to work*
>
> A recent study showed that <u>10% of the American workforce</u> is made up of self-employed workers. The self-employed then provide jobs for an additional (29 million) people.

3 As you read the text, annotate the important words, dates, numbers, and ideas.

4 Look at the headings. Which paragraph in the text does each one describe?

a Ideas and Creativity   Paragraph _____
b Goals Then and Now   Paragraph _____
c The Growth of Google   Paragraph _____

5 Read the questions and circle the correct answers.

1 How does Google help new businesses?
  a Google lets new businesses borrow money.
  b Google helps new businesses find customers.
2 Where was Google's first office?
  a in a garage
  b at Stanford University
3 What does Google want its employees to do?
  a share creative ideas with each other
  b work at night and sometimes on weekends
4 Who might benefit from a self-driving car?
  a people who have trouble seeing
  b people who drive long distances to work

THE STORY OF GOOGLE

1   Google is a huge technology company. It specializes in online advertising and searching, as well as other Internet-related products. Google was started by Larry Page and Sergey Brin. They met at Stanford University in 1995. Their **goal** was to organize all of the information on the Web. Today, their company **employs** more than 40,000 people around the world. The two **partners** created a company that made searching the Internet easy. Now they focus on three main areas. They make sure their search engine[1] is fast and smart so that people can find information easily. They develop products that let people work on different devices and in different places. They help new businesses **advertise** and find new customers.

2   Google grew very quickly. Page and Brin registered[2] the domain name[3] Google.com in 1997. In 1998, they **set up** a small **office** in a garage and hired their first employee, Craig Silverstein. They **ran** their business in the garage until they could move to a larger space. In the busy years that followed, Google expanded its services. In 2000, people could do Internet searches in 15 languages, including Dutch, Chinese, and Korean. Today, people can search in more than 150,000 languages. Google **introduced** a map service in 2005 called Google Maps™. The same year, it came out with a program called Google Earth™. This program allowed users to see close-up pictures of cities and neighborhoods when they typed in an address. In 2006, the name "Google" became a verb in English dictionaries. This shows the company's influence on modern life.

3   Today, Google is a creative workplace where employees share ideas with each other. Page and Brin are available during the week to talk with their employees and answer questions. This open environment has resulted in many new ideas. In 2011, the company released a program called Google Art Project™ that helped people explore the world's top museums from their computer. As of 2017, Google was continuing its work on a self-driving car. In the future, this car could help people who can't see well to drive. The company extends its services to the community, too. In 2008, it started a yearly art contest for students. Every year, the winner's artwork appears on its homepage for one day. Google believes that creativity is important, both in the workplace and in the community. In addition to producing famous Internet products, Google gives people opportunities to be creative, which leads to success.

[1]**search engine** (n) a website used for finding specific information on the Internet

[2]**register** (v) put information on an official list

[3]**domain name** (n) the part of an email address or website address that shows the name of the organization that the address belongs to

6 Write *T* (true) or *F* (false) next to the statements. Then correct the false statements.

_____ **1** Google's only focus is on making their search engine smart and fast.

_____

_____ **2** In 2006, "Google" was added to dictionaries as a verb.

_____

_____ **3** The original Google partners answer questions their employees may have.

_____

_____ **4** Google released a program that teaches people how to draw famous works of art.

_____

7 Look at the events from the Google business story in the table.

1 In column A, write the year of each event.
2 In column B, number the events in the order that they happened.

	A year	B event
a Google searches could be done in 15 languages.		
b Google started an art contest for students.		
c The partners registered the domain name Google.com.		
d Google introduced a map program.		

READING BETWEEN THE LINES

8 What do you think the creators of Google believe? Circle the correct answer.

a It is necessary to be creative if you want to be successful.
b Creativity is not important.

9 In which paragraph did you find the answer? _____

DISCUSSION

10 Discuss the questions with a partner.

1 Do you think Google's partners knew how successful they would become?
2 Would you like to have your own business? Why or why not?
3 If you had your own business, what would it be?

11 Work with a partner. Use ideas from Reading 1 and Reading 2 to answer the questions.

1 Look again at the quiz in Reading 1. What type of person would fit into the culture of Google?

2 Would you like to work at a large company like Google? Why or why not?

⊙ LANGUAGE DEVELOPMENT

COLLOCATIONS WITH *BUSINESS*

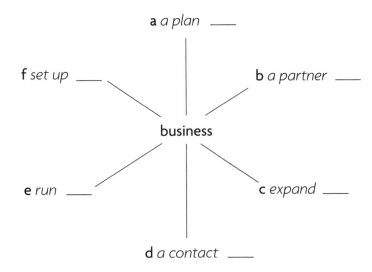

1 The words in the diagram are collocations of *business*. Write *N* next to the nouns and *V* next to the verbs.

2 Use words from the diagram to complete the sentences.

1 **A business** _____ is a detailed document describing the future plans of a business.

2 _____ **a business** means to make a business bigger.

3 **A business** _____ is a person who owns a business with you.

4 _____ **a business** means to be in charge of and control a business.

5 _____ **a business** means to start a business.

6 **A business** _____ is a person you know because of your job.

3 Look at the sentences in Exercise 2 again and answer the questions.

1 Do the verbs go before or after the word *business*? _____

2 Do the nouns go before or after the word *business*? _____

BUSINESS VOCABULARY

4 Match the words to their definitions.

1	employ	**a**	a type of computer program
2	employee	**b**	to give someone a job
3	office	**c**	a place where people work
4	software	**d**	something a business makes to sell
5	product	**e**	a worker

5 Use the words from Exercise 4 to complete the email. You may need to use the plural form of some words.

To: Whole Company
From: James Curry
Subject: Important information

Important information for all (1)_____ of Jenson Co.

I am pleased to tell you that we are moving into a bright

new (2)_____ in three months. We are also getting

new (3)_____ for our computers. We will have more

space, so we can (4)_____ more people. I am very

confident that these changes will help us sell more of our

excellent (5)_____ .

Best,

James Curry

WRITING

CRITICAL THINKING

At the end of this unit, you are going to write a narrative paragraph. Look at this unit's Writing Task below.

> Write a narrative paragraph about the history of a business.

1 Look back at Reading 2 on page 133. Which years in the text were important for Google? Choose 2–3 important events.

▲ EVALUATE

1 _____

2 _____

3 _____

2 Discuss the years you chose with a partner.

> **SKILLS**
>
> ### Using a timeline to put past events in order
>
> When writing about things that happened in the past, writers usually put them in chronological order. That means you start with the event that happened first and end with the event that happened last. Timelines are a useful way to organize past events in chronological order.

3 Use the notes and annotations you made in Reading 2 to place the events below in Google's history in the correct place on the timeline. Write the dates above the timeline and the events below it.

APPLY ▲

```
1995  ____   ____   ____   ____   ____   ____
  |      |      |      |      |      |      |
  d
```

a Google Earth™ and Google Maps™ are launched.
b Google employs its first worker, Craig Silverstein.
c Page and Brin register the domain name Google.com.
d ~~Larry Page and Sergey Brin meet at Stanford University.~~
e Google starts its student art contest.
f "Google" becomes a verb in English dictionaries.
g It becomes possible to search Google in 15 languages.
h Google Art Project™ is launched.

4 Look up information about a business you are interested in. Find information about the business online. Write key dates and events on the timeline below.

5 Write the main facts in time order in the paragraph planner. Keep notes on other information and key details about the company. You will use this information for the Writing Task at the end of this unit.

Main fact 1	
Detail	
Main fact 2	
Detail	
Main fact 3	
Detail	
Main fact 4	
Detail	

GRAMMAR FOR WRITING

THE SIMPLE PRESENT AND THE SIMPLE PAST

LANGUAGE

Use the *simple present* to talk about events that happen in the present or to talk about a general truth.
The company **employs** more than 40,000 people around the world.

Use the *simple past* to talk about events that happened in the past.
The two partners **created** a company that **made** searching the Internet easy.

1 Circle the verbs in the sentences. Write *past* next to the verbs in the simple past and *present* next to the verbs in the simple present.

1 Ford is one of the most famous motor companies in the world.
2 Jacques Nasser joined Ford in 1968.
3 Jacques Nasser is the son of Abdo Nasser.
4 On January 1, 1999, Jacques Nasser became president of Ford.
5 In 2000, Ford bought Land Rover.
6 In 2003, Ford celebrated its 100th birthday.

PRISM Online Workbook

2 Circle the correct form of the verbs in the paragraph.

> The JLX company (1)*sells / sold* food to supermarkets and stores. In 2009, Michael Underwood (2)*sets up / set up* the business. In 2010, the company (3)*does / did* very well. In June, Michael Underwood (4)*employs / employed* three new employees. The company (5)*expands / expanded* and (6)*opens / opened* new offices in Europe. Today, JLX (7)*is / was* a very successful business.

3 Write the correct form of the verbs in parentheses. Use the simple past or simple present.

1 Nissan _____ (be) a Japanese company.
2 In 1824, John Cadbury _____ (open) the first Cadbury's chocolate shop.
3 Lego _____ (sell) toys.
4 Today, Nestlé _____ (be) the world's biggest food and drinks business.
5 Nokia _____ (start) in 1865.
6 In 1995, Amazon _____ (sell) the first book on Amazon.com.
7 Adidas _____ (make) sports clothes around the world.
8 In 1926, Mercedes-Benz _____ (design) its first car.

TIME CLAUSES WITH *WHEN* TO DESCRIBE PAST EVENTS

Use *when* with a time clause to describe the date or time that something happened in the past.
He started the business **when** he was sixteen.

To make the time of the event more important, put the time clause with *when* first and follow it with a comma.
When he was sixteen, he started the business.

PRISM Online Workbook

4 Rewrite the sentences using time clauses with *when*.

1 She became the CEO. She was 30.

_____

2 They employed six new workers. The business expanded.

_____

3 He left his job. He was 65.

_____

4 The store closed. The economy crashed.

_____

5 They expanded the company. It was still successful.

_____

ADDING DETAILS TO MAIN FACTS

In a narrative paragraph, adding details to the main facts makes the writing more interesting and informative. Giving examples and reasons, explaining ideas, and using adjectives are ways to add details.

The details should help your readers form a picture of the events in their minds. Ask yourself these questions to help add details to narrative writing:

- Who is the paragraph about?
- Why did the events happen?
- How can I help the reader make a mental picture of what I am describing?
- Can I make any information more specific with dates, reasons, adjectives, or examples?
- Do the details in my narrative tell the story?

1 Read about the history of YouTube. The sentences below the text add more details. Write the letters of the sentences in the correct places in the paragraph.

PRISM Online Workbook

> In 2005, three friends, Chad Hurley, Steve Chen, and Jawed Karim, had an idea for an Internet business. (1)_____ They created YouTube™. Today, YouTube is the second largest search engine on the Internet, and has over a billion users. YouTube's first office was located in a simple room. (2)_____ Their first video was posted in April 2005. It was called "Me at the Zoo." (3)_____ Within five months, over a million people saw the video. Businesses began to notice YouTube and wanted to advertise on the website. In July 2006, 65,000 new videos were posted every day. In November 2006, Google bought YouTube. (4)_____

a They wanted to help people share videos on the Internet.
b It showed Karim at the zoo talking about elephants.
c They paid the incredible price of $1.65 billion.
d The room was located above a pizza restaurant in Menlo Park, CA.

2 Look back at the completed timeline in Critical Thinking, Exercise 3. Write the letter of the main facts in the Google story timeline next to the matching details below.

1 Google Earth™ is a map that shows close-up pictures of cities and neighborhoods. _____
2 They are both students. Larry is 22 and Sergey is 21. _____
3 Craig is a student at Stanford University. _____
4 Contest winners' artwork appears on Google's homepage for one day each year. _____
5 Google.com becomes one of the most frequently used websites in the world. _____
6 These languages include Dutch, Chinese, and Korean. _____
7 People can explore the world's top museums from their computers. _____
8 It is a verb that means "to look for something on the Internet." _____

WRITING TASK

PRISM Online Workbook

> Write a narrative paragraph about the history of a business.

PLAN

1 Look back at your timeline and your notes about the company you did research on in Critical Thinking. Add any new information to your notes.

2 Write a topic sentence that explains what you are going to write about.

_____

_____

3 Think of some interesting details that will help you write your narrative paragraph. Under each main fact in the paragraph planner from Exercise 5 in Critical Thinking, add details such as dates, adjectives, reasons, and examples that can make the information more interesting and paint a picture for the reader.

4 Refer to the Task Checklist on page 143 as you prepare your paragraph.

WRITE A FIRST DRAFT

5 Write a first draft of your paragraph.

REVISE

6 Use the Task Checklist to review your paragraph for content and structure.

TASK CHECKLIST	✔
Did you write about the history of a business?	
Did you write about four main facts in time order?	
Did you give the date or time that the events happened?	
Did you add details to the main facts?	

7 Make any necessary changes to your paragraph.

EDIT

8 Use the Language Checklist to edit your paragraph for language errors.

LANGUAGE CHECKLIST	✔
Did you use the correct collocations with *business*?	
Did you use the correct forms of the simple present and the simple past?	
Did you use time clauses with *when* correctly?	

9 Make any necessary changes to your paragraph.

ON CAMPUS

CREATING CHECKLISTS

SKILLS

College students always have a lot of things to do. It can be hard to remember all the tasks. It can also feel like there is too much to do. Organized students create checklists to help them.

PREPARING TO READ

1 Work with a partner. Discuss the questions.

   1 Do you ever feel like you have too much to do? If so, what do you do to stay organized?

   2 Do you ever forget to do things? What kinds of things do you forget?

WHILE READING

2 Read about three students and their checklists.

Karl

I'm very organized. I make a checklist for the week every Monday. On a sheet of paper, I draw a box for each of my classes. In each box, I write all the tasks for that class in the week. If it's important, I draw a red star next to it. There is also one box for other tasks, like getting a new driver's license or buying socks.

COMMUNICATIONS 312

☐ review Chapter 12 for quiz *

☐ group project meeting: choose photos for slide show

TO-DO

☐ get concert tickets

☐ return books to library

Hiroo

I make a short checklist every day. I write down things like study group meetings or homework that I need to do that day. I like a short list. Everything on the list is important. I write the list on a sticky note and put it in my notebook. I'm really busy, so it helps me remember things.

• contact advisor about spring classes

• turn in essay by 5 p.m.

• return library books

Anya
We have lots of big projects in my design class, so I like to make checklists on my phone. I write down all the little tasks in the project. Then it seems easier because I can do all of those small things.

.ıll 4G   9:47 AM

TO-DO LIST
- ✔ Visit site with team 3/12
- ☐ Decide on plants
- ☐ Decide on material
- ☐ First drawing
- ☐ Revise drawing, due 5/1

3 Match the person (Karl, Hiroo, or Anya) to the statements.

1 Makes a short list of important things each day. _____
2 Keeps a checklist of many small things for a large project. _____
3 Writes checklists for each class every week. _____
4 Uses a phone for checklists. _____
5 Makes a list on a sticky note. _____

PRACTICE

4 Create three checklists: *American Literature 112*, *Math 114*, and a *To-do* list. Put the tasks in the correct checklist.

buy plane ticket	make dentist appointment
do Problem Set 4	get haircut
write summary of short story	choose novel for final paper
library: get information about author	review algebra formulas for midterm

REAL-WORLD APPLICATION

5 Choose one of your classes. List four tasks for that class. Draw a star next to the most important task(s).

6 Share your checklist with a partner.

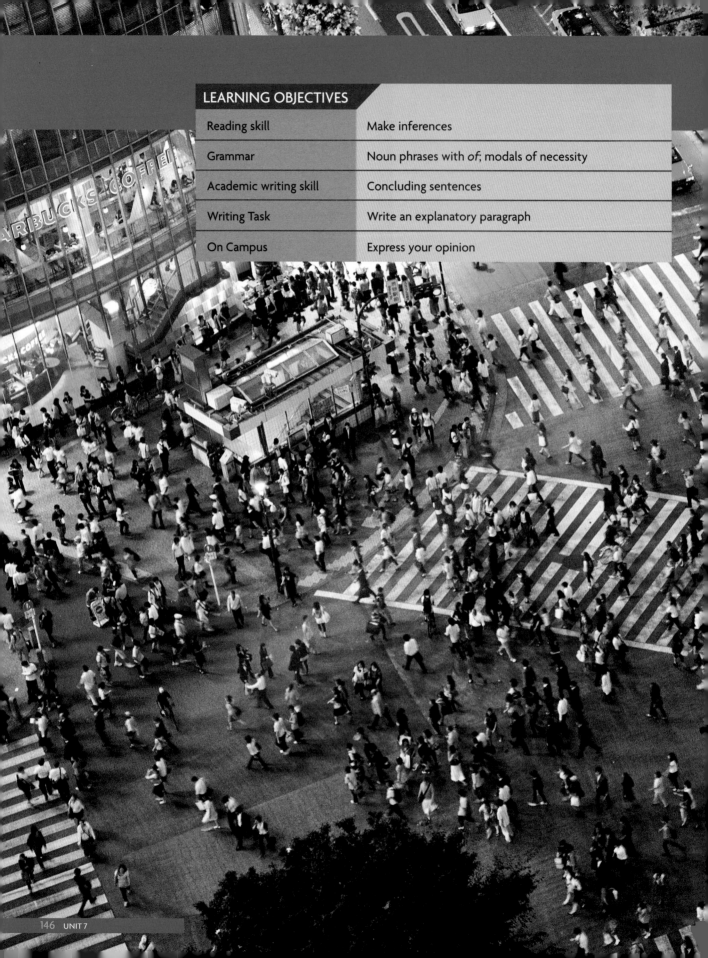

LEARNING OBJECTIVES

Reading skill	Make inferences
Grammar	Noun phrases with *of*; modals of necessity
Academic writing skill	Concluding sentences
Writing Task	Write an explanatory paragraph
On Campus	Express your opinion

ACTIVATE YOUR KNOWLEDGE

Look at the photos and answer the questions.

1 What are the names of the people?
2 What did they do to become famous?

WATCH AND LISTEN

PREPARING TO WATCH

ACTIVATING YOUR
KNOWLEDGE

1 Work with a partner and answer the questions.

   1 What is a volunteer?
   2 Why do people become volunteers?
   3 Where do volunteers work?

PREDICTING CONTENT
USING VISUALS

2 You are going to watch a video about a volunteer. Work with your partner. Look at the pictures from the video. What kind of work do you think the man is doing?

> **GLOSSARY**
>
> **observer** (n) someone whose job is to watch people or events
>
> **monitor** (v) to watch something to make sure that it is correct
>
> **National Weather Service** (n) the part of the U.S. government that provides weather forecasts and warnings of dangerous weather
>
> **honor** (v) to show great respect for someone or something
>
> **statistic** (n) a fact in the form of a number that shows information about something

WHILE WATCHING

3 ▶ Read the sentences. Then watch the video. Write *T* (true) or *F* (false). Correct the false statements.

UNDERSTANDING MAIN IDEAS

_____ 1 850 volunteers record the weather in the U.S. every day.
_____

_____ 2 Richard Hendrickson is a volunteer for the National Weather Service.
_____

_____ 3 He monitors the temperature from his kitchen.
_____

_____ 4 This job is difficult for him.
_____

_____ 5 Richard also checks the snowfall daily.
_____

_____ 6 He uses his cell phone to call the National Weather Service.
_____

_____ 7 The National Weather Service will honor him for his time as a volunteer.
_____

4 ▶ Watch again. Choose the correct answer.

UNDERSTANDING DETAILS

1 Richard Hendrickson is _____ years old.
  a 85   **b** 90   **c** 101
2 He lives in _____ , New York.
  a Bridgehampton   **b** Brooklyn   **c** Long Beach
3 He started recording the weather in _____ .
  a 1925   **b** 1930   **c** 1940
4 Weather was important to him because he was _____ .
  a an engineer   **b** a farmer   **c** a teacher

5 Work with a partner. Discuss the questions.

MAKING INFERENCES

  1 Why does Richard like being a volunteer?
  2 Why do you think Richard first became a volunteer?
  3 Will he stop volunteering for the National Weather Service?

DISCUSSION

6 Work in small groups. Discuss the questions. Explain your answers.

  1 What kind of volunteer work have you done or would you like to do?
  2 What kind of volunteer work would you not like to do?
  3 What are five personal benefits of being a volunteer?

READING

READING 1

UNDERSTANDING KEY VOCABULARY

PREPARING TO READ

1 Read the definitions. Complete the sentences with the correct form of the words in bold.

> **blind** (adj) not able to see
>
> **incredible** (adj) impossible or very difficult to believe; amazing
>
> **inspire** (v) to make other people feel that they want to do something
>
> **operation** (n) the process when doctors cut your body to repair it or to take something out
>
> **respect** (v) to like or to have a very good opinion of someone because of their knowledge, achievements, etc.
>
> **talent** (n) a natural ability to do something well

1 After the _____ on his foot, Alex had to stay in the hospital until he could walk on his own.
2 Liz Murray went to Harvard, and then became a best-selling author. What is _____ is that she was homeless only a few years before she went to Harvard.
3 Julia was _____ when she was born, so she could not see. Her parents taught her words by putting objects in her hands so she could touch them.
4 Fernanda had a special _____ for playing the piano. She could listen to a song and then play it almost perfectly without any practice.
5 Mahatma Gandhi did a lot of important things for the people of India. I really _____ him and everything he did for people.
6 Having more examples of women as CEOs of businesses will _____ more young girls to reach for similar goals.

SCANNING TO PREDICT CONTENT

2 Read the title and the first sentence in each paragraph in the blog post on page 151. What do you think the blog post will be about?

a someone who helped people with cancer
b someone who was blind and trained to be a doctor
c someone who was blind but learned how to see

3 Read the blog post and check your answer to Exercise 2.

INCREDIBLE PEOPLE

/2017//Ben Underwood

1 Ben Underwood was a normal teenage boy. He loved playing basketball, riding his bicycle, listening to music with his friends, and playing video games. But in one way, Ben was different from most other teenagers—he was blind. However, Ben had a special **talent**. He didn't have eyes, but he could still "see."

2 Ben was born on January 26, 1992. For the first two years of his life, Ben was a happy and healthy baby. He had a normal life, living with his mother and two older brothers in California. However, when Ben was two years old, his life changed. In 1994, he was taken to the hospital because he had problems with his eyes. The doctors looked at his eyes and told his mother the bad news—Ben had cancer[1]. After a few months, he had an **operation** to remove the cancer. The operation was successful, and Ben was fine. However, the doctors had to remove his eyes, and Ben became **blind**.

3 After his operation, Ben developed an **incredible** talent. When he was three, he learned how to "see" buildings with his ears. He listened very carefully, and he could hear noises bounce off buildings. The noises told him where the buildings were. Then, when Ben was seven, he learned to "click." He made clicking noises with his mouth, and listened for the noises that bounced back from things. In this way, Ben could "see" where he was and what was around him. This is the same way dolphins see things underwater and bats see in the dark.

4 Scientists and doctors were amazed by Ben's talent. There are only a few blind people in the world who can see like Ben. People **respected** him because of this. He became famous. He was on TV, and he traveled to different countries and talked to people about his life. Sadly, when Ben was 16, his cancer came back. He died soon after. However, during Ben's life, he taught people that anything is possible. Many people admired him because he **inspired** them and helped them feel strong. When he died in 2009, over 2,000 people went to his funeral.

[1]**cancer** (n) a serious disease that makes people very sick because cells in the body grow in ways that are not normal or controlled

WHILE READING

4 Read the blog post again. Write the paragraph number where you can find the information below.

a Ben learned to "see" again. Paragraph: _____

b Ben was an ordinary boy, but he could do something amazing.
Paragraph: _____

c Ben became a hero for many people. Paragraph: _____

d Ben became ill and lost his eyes. Paragraph: _____

5 Read the blog post again and write *T* (true) or *F* (false) next to the statements. Correct the false statements.

_____ **1** Ben liked playing basketball.

_____

_____ **2** Ben was just like other teenagers.

_____

_____ **3** Ben learned to "see" by touching things.

_____

_____ **4** Ben couldn't ride a bicycle.

_____

_____ **5** Ben had two older brothers.

_____

_____ **6** Ben liked listening to music.

_____

6 Put the events in Ben's life in the correct order on the timeline.

a Ben learned how to "see" buildings with his ears.

b Ben was born.

c Ben learned how to "click."

d Ben's cancer came back.

e Ben had a problem with his eyes.

f Ben died.

g Ben went on a TV show.

READING BETWEEN THE LINES

WORKING OUT MEANING

7 Look at the underlined words in the text. Then look at the sentence below and circle the word that is a synonym for the word in bold.

I really **admire** her. She's an excellent teacher.

a dislike
b respect
c employ

IDENTIFYING PURPOSE

8 Circle the correct answer.

1 Who do you think wrote the blog?
   a a scientist
   b a journalist
2 Why do you think the author wrote this blog?
   a to teach doctors about cancer
   b to tell people the story of Ben's life

DISCUSSION

9 Think of another famous child or teenager and discuss the questions with a partner.

1 What is his/her name? How old is he/she?
2 Why is he/she famous?
3 How is his/her life different from other children's or teenagers' lives? Think about the list below.
   • school
   • hobbies
   • friends
   • home

PREPARING TO READ

1 You are going to read blog posts about incredible people. Read the sentences and write the words in bold next to the correct definitions.

1 My mom thinks I'm too young to **take care of** my little sister, so a babysitter comes to my house every day.

2 My **former** job was boring because I sat at my computer all day. At my current job, I talk to a lot of customers, and I like that much better.

3 Aisha runs at least ten miles (16 kilometers) every morning to **train** for the upcoming race.

4 It is important for a president to be **honest**. People must be able to trust the person leading their country.

5 People say Terence Tao is one of the most **intelligent** people in the world. He earned a Ph.D. at only age 20 and became a math professor at age 24.

6 Eugene was **brave** when he ran into a burning house to save an elderly woman. He could have died, but he did it anyway.

7 After five tries, 64-year-old Diana Nyad was finally able to **achieve** her goal of swimming from Cuba to Florida. It took her almost 53 hours to finish the 100-mile (160-kilometer) swim.

8 William graduated from college and then decided to follow his **dream** of opening a restaurant.

a _____ (n) something that you really want to do, be, or have in the future

b _____ (phr v) to care for or be responsible for someone or something

c _____ (adj) not afraid of dangerous or difficult situations

d _____ (adj) before the present time or in the past

e _____ (adj) able to learn and understand things easily; smart

f _____ (v) to prepare for a job, activity, or sport by learning skills or by exercise

g _____ (adj) truthful or able to be trusted; not likely to lie, cheat, or steal

h _____ (v) to succeed in doing something difficult

INCREDIBLE PEOPLE

/Steve Jobs

1 I really admire Steve Jobs, the **former** CEO of Apple. He invented a new kind of technology. Apple technology is very **intelligent**, but it is also easy to use. The products that he made are also really beautiful. Steve Jobs is a good role model[1] because he was an excellent businessman. He worked hard, and he created a successful business in IT. I was very sad when he died in October 2011. I respect him because he changed the way people use technology all over the world.

Ahmed Aziz, _____

/Mary Evans

2 My mom, Mary Evans, is my role model. I have a very big family, with two brothers and three sisters. My mom works very hard every day to **take care of** us, and she is very busy. She always makes time for everyone, and she always listens to me if I have a problem. She gives me advice, and she is always right. I have a nephew who is sick and has to go to the hospital a lot. My mom often sleeps at the hospital with him. I really respect her because she always takes care of my family and makes sure that we have everything we need.

Mark Evans, _____

/Singapore Women's Everest Team

3 My role models are the Singapore Women's Everest Team. In 2009, they became the first all-women team to climb Mount Everest. The team of six young women **trained** for seven years before they climbed the mountain. It was difficult for them to train because Singapore doesn't have any snow or mountains. But they didn't stop, and in the end they **achieved** their goal. They worked hard every day for their **dream**, so I really admire them.

Li Chan, _____

/Malala Yousafzai

4 Malala Yousafzai is a **brave** and **honest** young woman. In Pakistan, the Taliban didn't let girls go to school. Malala went anyway. She wrote a blog for the BBC describing the terrible things the Taliban were doing. In 2012, two men came onto her school bus and shot her in the head. Luckily, Malala survived. She gave speeches about the millions of girls around the world who were not allowed to go to school. In 2014, Malala won the Nobel Peace Prize. She donated her $1.1 million prize money to build a school for girls in Pakistan. Malala is a good role model because she is brave, she never gives up, and she tells the truth no matter what.

Jane Kloster, _____

[1]**role model** (n) someone you try to behave like because you admire them

WHILE READING

2 Read the blog posts on page 155. Match the sentence halves.

1	Steve Jobs	**a**	takes care of her family.
2	Mary Evans	**b**	fights for girls to go to school.
3	The Singapore Women's Everest Team	**c**	invented a new kind of technology.
4	Malala Yousafzai	**d**	climbed a mountain.

3 Look at the sentences. There is one mistake in each one. Correct the false information.

1 In 2009, the Singapore Women's Everest team climbed Everest after five years of training.

_____

2 Malala Yousafzai donated $1.1 million to build a library in Pakistan.

_____

3 Steve Jobs died in June 2011.

_____

4 Mark's mother takes care of his grandmother in the hospital.

_____

READING BETWEEN THE LINES

Making inferences

Good readers make inferences about a text. To make an inference, think about what the author writes, how he or she writes it, and what you already know about the subject to make a guess about information that is not in the text.

4 In the text on page 155, the jobs of the people writing the comments have been removed. Write the jobs of the writers next to their names.

a an explorer
b a teacher
c an IT technician
d an author

DISCUSSION

5 Discuss the questions with a partner.

1 Who are the most famous people in your country?
2 How can famous people inspire others to do good things?
3 Why do news services often write about famous people?

6 Use ideas from Reading 1 and Reading 2 to answer the questions.

  1 Do you want to be famous? Why or why not?

  2 Think about the people you read about in Reading 1 and Reading 2. Who do you share the most qualities with?

 ## LANGUAGE DEVELOPMENT

NOUN PHRASES WITH *OF*

> **LANGUAGE**
>
> You can use the word *of* to join two nouns together and make a noun phrase.
> He is the president **of** the country.
> He invented a type **of** technology.
> We write a conclusion at the end **of** an essay.

PRISM Online Workbook

1 Match the sentence halves.

1	A chair is	a	the principal of the school.
2	I travel to	b	the beginning of the day.
3	A dog is	c	a kind of furniture.
4	Coffee is	d	a lot of countries.
5	Write your name at	e	a sort of drink.
6	My teacher is	f	the top of the page.
7	We eat breakfast at	g	a type of animal.

2 Put the words in order to make complete sentences.

  1 the new leader / She / of / the country / is / .

  _____

  2 of / I met / my brother's / a friend / .

  _____

  3 gave me / of / a piece / My mother / cake / .

  _____

  4 a kind / A dentist / doctor / is / of / .

  _____

  5 of / the former director / is / technology / He / .

  _____

ADJECTIVES TO DESCRIBE PEOPLE

3 Are the adjectives in the box positive or negative? Write the words in the correct place in the table. Some answers may fit in both columns. Use a dictionary to look up any words you don't know.

> reliable   confident   lazy   honest   calm   talented
> kind   shy   intelligent   patient   stupid
> clever   difficult   sensible   selfish   friendly

positive	negative

4 Use adjectives from Exercise 3 to complete the sentences.

1 Luka is very _____ . He always tells the truth.
2 My teacher is _____ . She is very relaxed and doesn't get worried or angry.
3 She always chats with students in other classes. She's so _____ .
4 She doesn't talk very much. She's really _____ .
5 James hasn't done anything all day. He's so _____ .
6 Ahmed is very _____ . He always comes to work on time and does his job.
7 Dae-Jung is practical and doesn't do anything stupid. He's very _____ .
8 He is a very _____ driver. He wins every race easily.

WRITING

CRITICAL THINKING

At the end of this unit, you will write an explanatory paragraph. Look at this unit's Writing Task below.

> Who do you think is a good role model? Write a paragraph explaining the qualities that make that person a good role model.

APPLY

SKILLS

Using a Venn diagram

A *Venn diagram* has two circles that overlap in the middle. Writers use Venn diagrams to think about the similarities between people or ideas. Venn diagrams help organize the qualities that people or ideas share. To complete a Venn diagram, write the shared qualities of people or ideas in the overlapping section of the circles.

1 Work with a partner. Choose two people from Reading 2 to compare. Complete the Venn diagram to find the shared qualities of the people. Think about adjectives that describe them and the things these people have done.

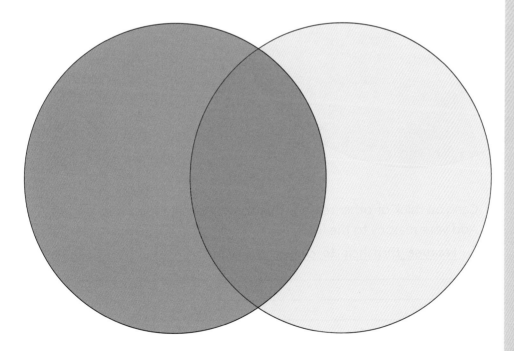

2 Read the four reasons why the people in Reading 2 are role models. Write the name of the person next to the reason. More than one answer is possible.

a because they are good at sports _____

b because they help people _____

c because they are intelligent _____

d because they were head of a company _____

3 Think of two of your own role models. Write lists of their qualities.

4 Complete the Venn diagram to find the shared qualities of the two role models you chose.

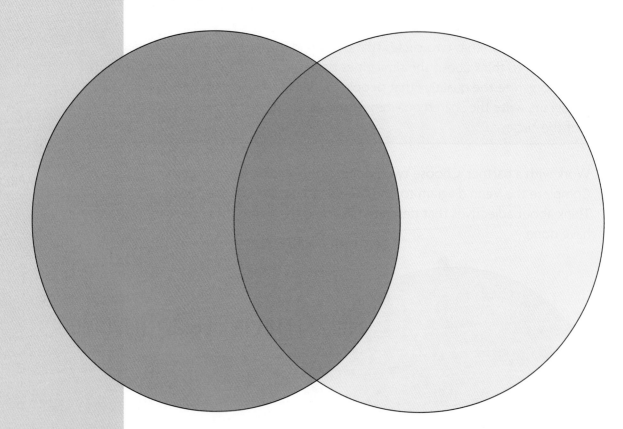

5 Can you think of other reasons that someone might be a role model? Add your reasons to the list.

1 _because they help to change the world_____

2 _____

3 _____

4 _____

6 Choose one of the role models from the Venn diagram in Exercise 4. Why is he or she a good role model?

7 Think of four more things that this person has done that makes him or her a good role model, and add them to the Venn diagram in Exercise 4.

GRAMMAR FOR WRITING

MODALS OF NECESSITY

> LANGUAGE
>
> *Should*, *have to*, and *must* express what is required, necessary, or strongly suggested.
> A role model **should** inspire people.
> Role models **have to** set a good example for others.
> A role model **must** be kind.
>
> The negative forms are *should not*, *do / does not have to*, and *must not*.
> A good role model **should not / must not** be lazy.
> People don't **have to** be rich to be good role models.
>
> In academic writing, use the modal *should* or the phrase *it is important to* to say what you believe is the right or best thing to do.
> **It is important to** stay in school.
> We **should** spend more time helping others.

1 Which of these things should good role models be or do? Write sentences using *should*, *must*, *have to*, or *should not*, *must not*, *do not have to*. Use the phrases in parentheses.

Good role models should be sensible.

1 (work hard)

_____

2 (be selfish)

_____

3 (ask others what they need)

_____

4 (be patient)

_____

5 (be mean to others)

_____

PRISM Online Workbook

2 Which of these things are important for role models? Write two sentences using *it is important to*. Use the phrases in parentheses.

1 (be patient)

_____

2 (spend time with your family)

_____

3 (learn about other people)

_____

4 (get a good education)

_____

5 (be reliable)

_____

3 Compare and discuss your answers with a partner. Do you agree or disagree? Why?

ACADEMIC WRITING SKILLS

CONCLUDING SENTENCES

The *concluding sentence* is the last sentence in a paragraph. The concluding sentence gives your opinion and repeats the main idea of the paragraph using different words. Writers sometimes use phrases such as *in conclusion*, *in summary*, or *in short* to begin concluding sentences.

1 Look at the two sentences. Which one is a concluding sentence?

a In summary, I admire my mother because she is kind.
b First, she always takes care of my family.

2 Underline the phrase in Exercise 1 that shows you it is a concluding sentence.

3 What type of punctuation follows the phrase you underlined?

a a period
b a comma

4 Match the topic sentences to the concluding sentences.

Topic sentences

1 I really admire my teacher, Mrs. Franklin. _____
2 My parents care for my family. _____
3 Professional soccer players have to train every day. _____
4 My uncle is my hero. _____

Concluding sentences

a In conclusion, I admire him a lot.
b In short, it is difficult to compete against other teams if you don't practice.
c In summary, they work hard to make sure my brothers and I have everything we need.
d In short, I respect her because she works so hard at the school.

5 Read the paragraph and circle the best concluding sentence.

> Samantha Cristoforetti has been very successful in life so far. She studied mechanical engineering in Germany. Then she joined the Air Force in Italy, her home country. She became a captain. In 2009, Samantha became an astronaut. In 2015, she lived in space for almost 200 days. During her time in space, she posted a lot of beautiful pictures and interacted with people on social media.

a In short, Samantha Cristoforetti still has more that she wants to learn.
b In conclusion, Samantha Cristoforetti has accomplished a lot in her life.
c In summary, Samantha Cristoforetti enjoys using social media.

Samantha Cristoforetti

PRISM Online Workbook

Who do you think is a good role model? Write a paragraph explaining the qualities that make that person a good role model.

PLAN

1 Write a topic sentence to introduce the person you chose and explain why you think he or she is a good role model.

... is a good role model because ...

_____

_____

2 Look at the Venn diagram you made in Exercise 4 of Critical Thinking. Use the shared qualities of the two people as examples of what makes a person a good role model. Write the qualities and examples in the order you will write about them in your paragraph. What are some of the qualities that are special for the person you chose?

1 _____

_____

2 _____

_____

3 _____

_____

4 _____

_____

3 Write a concluding sentence that repeats your main idea in different words. Use phrases like *in conclusion*, *in summary*, or *in short* to show that this is the concluding sentence.

_____

_____

4 Refer to the Task Checklist on page 165 as you prepare your paragraph.

WRITE A FIRST DRAFT

5 Write the first draft of your paragraph.

REVISE

6 Use the Task Checklist to review your paragraph for content and structure.

TASK CHECKLIST	✔
Did you write about your role model?	
Did you write about why the person is your role model?	
Does your paragraph have a topic sentence, supporting sentences, and a concluding sentence?	
Does your concluding sentence give your opinion and repeat the main idea of the paragraph?	

7 Make any necessary changes to your paragraph.

EDIT

8 Use the Language Checklist to edit your paragraph for language errors.

LANGUAGE CHECKLIST	✔
Did you use noun phrases with *of* correctly?	
Did you use adjectives to describe people correctly?	
Did you use *should*, *have to*, and *must* correctly?	
Did you use *it is important to* correctly?	

9 Make any necessary changes to your paragraph.

ON CAMPUS

EXPRESSING YOUR OPINION

In classes and in online discussions, college students often give their opinions. They can disagree with their classmates, but it is important to be polite.

PREPARING TO READ

1 Work with a partner. Discuss the questions.

1 Are you afraid to disagree with a classmate on a discussion board?
2 How do you feel when people disagree with your opinion?
3 What are some polite ways to disagree with someone?

WHILE READING

2 Read these posts from a class discussion board. Then match the names below to the opinions.

> **Question:** Should all high school students have to wear school uniforms?
>
> **Erica:** In my opinion, uniforms are not good for high school students. They should be able to choose their own clothes. Clothes are important for teenagers because they want to have their own style. _Posted 15m ago_
>
> **Renee:** That's a good point, Erica. However, I feel uniforms are better for everyone. Some students can afford nice clothes, but some students can't buy those clothes. I believe uniforms make everyone the same at school. _Posted 8m ago_
>
> **David:** I agree, Renee. I think school should be for studying, not for fashion. Erica, I see your point, but I don't really agree. Can't students wear their own clothes after school? _Posted 5m ago_

1 Erica	**a**	Students want to be fashionable.
2 Renee	**b**	Students should focus on schoolwork, not clothes.
3 David	**c**	Uniforms make students equal.

3 Choose the correct word for each sentence.

1 Erica believes students _should / should not_ wear uniforms in high school.
2 Renee _agrees / doesn't agree_ with Erica about school uniforms.
3 Renee _thinks / doesn't think_ that Erica makes a good point.
4 Renee _writes / doesn't write_ her own opinion.
5 David _understands / doesn't understand_ Erica's opinion.

4 Read the discussion again.

   1 Underline four phrases that start an opinion.

   2 Circle two phrases that show understanding of someone's opinion.

PRACTICE

5 Complete the sentences with correct words.

> agree   but   opinion   see   think

Question: Should high schools require music for all students?

Megan: For many reasons, I don't (1)_____ music classes should be required. First, it's not a necessary subject like math or science.
Second, schools don't have a lot of money. If students want to study music, they should take private lessons. In my (2)_____ , schools should not require music.

Posted 19m ago

Katie: I don't really (3)_____ . Music is important for all students.
I (4)_____ your point about money, (5)_____ students often buy or rent their own instruments. They also pay for their trips to competitions.

Posted 8m ago

6 Write your own short response to this question.

REAL-WORLD APPLICATION

7 Write 3–4 sentences to respond to one of the questions.

Respond to one of the following questions.

1	Do professional athletes make good role models?
2	Should junk food be banned in school cafeterias?
3	Is it OK to use cell phones in class?
4	At what age should people be allowed to drive?

8 Exchange your response with a partner. Write 2–3 sentences to respond to your partner's writing.

9 Share your responses with the class.

LEARNING OBJECTIVES

Reading skill	Identify the author's purpose
Grammar	*That* clauses in complex sentences; infinitives of purpose
Academic writing skill	Essay organization
Writing Task	Complete an opinion essay
On Campus	Use the library

ACTIVATE YOUR KNOWLEDGE

Look at the photo and answer the questions.

1 What is the person doing?

2 Why do governments send people to space?

3 Would you like to travel to space? Why or why not?

WATCH AND LISTEN

PREPARING TO WATCH

ACTIVATING YOUR KNOWLEDGE

1 Work with a partner and answer the questions.

1 How do people usually get to work when they live far from their workplace?
2 Why might people live far from their workplace?
3 What are some unusual offices or workplace?

USING YOUR KNOWLEDGE

2 You are going to watch a video about a woman who traveled to space for work. Write five adjectives and five nouns to describe a trip to space.

Adjectives: _____ , _____ , _____ , _____ , _____

Nouns: _____ , _____ , _____ , _____ , _____

> **GLOSSARY**
>
> **astronaut** (n) someone who travels to and works in space
>
> **International Space Station** (n) the name of an international spacecraft where astronauts work on projects
>
> **rocket** (n) a vehicle for traveling to space
>
> **capsule** (n) the part of the rocket where the astronauts are
>
> **blast off** (phr v) to leave the ground; for example, when a spacecraft or rocket blasts off, it leaves the ground.

WHILE WATCHING

3 ▶ Watch the video. Answer the questions.

1 What does Sunita Williams do?

_____

2 What is the name of her office in space?

_____

3 How did she get there?

_____

4 What was not a problem when she went there?

_____

5 What took longer, her trip to space or her drive to work?

_____

UNDERSTANDING
MAIN IDEAS

4 ▶ Watch again. Complete the sentences with the correct numbers.

1 It takes Sunita Williams _____ minutes to drive to the office.
2 She drives her car _____ miles to the office in Houston, Texas.
3 She spent _____ months in space.
4 The trip to space was _____ miles straight up.
5 The trip took _____ minutes.

UNDERSTANDING
DETAILS

5 Correct the mistakes in the student's notes. Compare your answers with a partner.

1 The rocket is American.

2 The trip took double the time it takes her to drive to work.

3 She traveled in a big capsule.

4 She went with a Russian cosmonaut and a Korean astronaut.

5 They rode the elevator to the bottom.

DISCUSSION

6 Work with a partner. Discuss the questions. Explain your answers.

1 What are the dangers of traveling to space?
2 What kind of person works in space?
3 What is "space tourism"? How do you feel about it?

READING

PREPARING TO READ

UNDERSTANDING KEY VOCABULARY

1 Read the sentences. Write the words in bold next to the definitions.

1 Mariam loves to **explore** new places. She even wants to travel to Mars one day to learn about it.
2 Thanks to developing technology, **advances** in science and medicine are made all the time.
3 Astronauts have not set foot **beyond** the moon, but one day soon they may go to planets that are farther away.
4 It is important for an **entrepreneur** to understand that they might lose all of their money if their new business fails.
5 The rocket **crashed** when it was landing. Luckily, the people inside were not hurt.
6 Tesla is a **private** company. The government does not run it.
7 Some people don't think we should use **public** money, like taxes, to pay for space travel. They think companies should pay for it.

a _____ (n) someone who starts their own business
b _____ (n) progress in the development or improvement of something
c _____ (adj) related to money or services controlled or supplied by a person or a company and not by the government
d _____ (v) to travel to a new place to learn about it
e _____ (prep) on the farther side of; at a farther distance than
f _____ (v) to hit something by accident, especially in a vehicle
g _____ (adj) related to money or services controlled or supplied by the government and not by a person or a company

USING YOUR KNOWLEDGE

2 You are going to read an article about space travel. Before you read, discuss the questions with a partner.

1 Who pays for space exploration?
2 Do you think people will ever vacation in space? Why or why not?

The Rise of Commercial[1] Space Travel

Elon Musk and *Dragon*

1   In 1957, the Soviet Union sent *Sputnik I* into space. It was the first successful spacecraft to orbit[2] the Earth, and it started the time period known as the Space Age. A short time later in the U.S., the National Aeronautics Space Administration (NASA) successfully sent another spacecraft, *Explorer I*, into space. In the years that followed, incredible **advances** were made. Astronauts orbited the Earth and men walked on the moon. The world, it seemed, wanted to learn what was **beyond** Earth.

2   Today, space exploration continues, and governments still compete with one another to make new discoveries. In 2012, NASA landed its unmanned[3] spacecraft *Curiosity* on Mars in order to collect information about the planet. In 2016, Europe and Russia worked together and sent a spacecraft to Mars. China and India are also working on similar projects. However, there has been one big change: **private** companies, instead of **public** government organizations, are entering the Space Race[4].

3   SpaceX has been very successful in commercial space travel. They designed the spacecraft *Dragon* in order to deliver supplies to the International Space Station (ISS). In 2012, *Dragon* was the first commercial spacecraft in history to do that. Elon Musk, the man who started the company, has dreams that go beyond making deliveries. He hopes that SpaceX will be able to send people to Mars by 2025.

4   Another **entrepreneur** who supports commercial space travel is Richard Branson. He started a private company called Virgin Galactic. Their goal is to open space travel to everyone. The company has sold almost 700 future trips to space, at the high cost of $250,000 per person. Those future space tourists come from countries all over the world and are all different ages.

5   Private companies are lucky in one way. They don't have to wait for money from the government like NASA does. However, that doesn't mean that setbacks[5] and accidents don't happen. In 2014, Virgin Galactic's *VSS Enterprise* **crashed** in the Mojave Desert during a test flight. The 39-year-old pilot, Michael Alsbury, was killed. In 2016, a SpaceX spacecraft that was going to the ISS exploded on the launch pad in Cape Canaveral, Florida. No one was hurt, but important supplies were lost.

6   The race to **explore** the universe continues, and many private companies are competing. Some of those companies want to take people to the moon and back someday. Others want to take people to Mars. The possibilities are endless. Maybe in our lifetime, those dreams will come true.

Richard Branson and a Virgin Galactic spacecraft

---

[1]**commercial** (adj) with the purpose of making money
[2]**orbit** (v) to travel in a circular journey around the sun, the moon, or a planet
[3]**unmanned** (adj) without people to operate something or make something work properly
[4]**Space Race** (n) the competition between countries to make advances in the field of space exploration
[5]**setbacks** (n) problems that make something happen later or more slowly than it should

WHILE READING

3 Read the text on page 173 and answer the questions.

1 What is the Space Age?
2 What are countries competing with one another for?
3 What are some goals of future space travel?
4 What is one difference between public and private companies?

4 Read the statements. Write *T* (true), *F* (false), or *DNS* (does not say). Then correct the false statements.

_____ 1 NASA sent *Sputnik I* into space, and it was the first successful spacecraft to orbit the Earth.

_____ 2 Entrepreneurs like Elon Musk and Richard Branson have to wait for government money in order to construct new spacecraft.

_____ 3 In 2016, a SpaceX spacecraft exploded in Cape Canaveral, Florida, and killed its pilot.

_____ 4 Virgin Galactic has sold nearly 500 future trips to space.

_____ 5 Elon Musk also runs an innovative car company.

READING BETWEEN THE LINES

Identifying the author's purpose

Authors write in order to inform, explain, entertain, or persuade readers. The author's purpose may be understood by his or her use of key words, tone, and language in the text. Good readers identify why a text was written. The author's purpose may be stated clearly in the text, or it may have to be inferred.

5 Read the text on page 173 again. Circle the correct answers.

1 The purpose of the text is to ...
   a persuade readers that commercial space travel is necessary.
   b inform readers about the advances in commercial space travel.
   c entertain readers about the possibility of life on Mars.

2 You could find the text in ...
   a a magazine.
   b a textbook.
   c a science fiction novel.

3 The author is ...
   a analyzing commercial space travel.
   b describing commercial space travel.
   c questioning the benefits of commercial space travel.

DISCUSSION

6 Discuss the questions with a partner.

1 Would you pay a lot of money to be a space tourist? Why or why not?

2 Why might some people want to leave Earth and live on Mars?

READING 2

PREPARING TO READ

UNDERSTANDING
KEY VOCABULARY

PRISM Online Workbook

1 Circle the best definition for each word in bold.

1 I often **wonder** if people will travel to Mars one day. Maybe NASA will send someone there in the next ten or fifteen years.

a think about something and try to understand it

b not believe something

2 My essay is weak because I didn't **support** my ideas with expert opinions. I should find more research to add to my essay.

a think of more topics to write about

b help show that something is true

3 A lot of **evidence** shows that Mars once had flowing water.

a opinions that people have about a topic

b something that makes you believe something is true

4 Scientists have been studying space for many years. Some think there is life on other planets, but no one can **prove** it.

a show that something is true

b ask questions about something

5 Life can't **exist** without air and water. For that reason, Earth is the perfect planet for life.

a be real, alive, or present

b have ideas

6 Because it was so difficult, Elise thought it was **unlikely** that she would pass her astronomy class.

a would probably happen

b not expected to happen; not probable

7 Astronauts have to train a lot in order to prepare for the **conditions** they'll face in space, such as very hot and very cold temperatures.

a the location of something

b the physical state that someone or something is in

8 On **particular** nights, you can see the brightest planets when you look at the sky. That only happens when the sky is clear.

a used to talk about one thing or person and not others

b many different

2 Read the title of the text on page 177. What type of text is it?

  a a story

  b an essay

  c a newspaper article

WHILE READING

3 Read the text again and write the number of the paragraphs where the author mentions each idea.

  a There is not enough evidence to prove that Kepler 22b has life.
Paragraph: _____

  b Earth is the only planet with the right conditions for life.
Paragraph: _____

  c There are arguments for and against the idea that life exists on other planets. Paragraph: _____

  d It is unlikely that there is life on another planet because the conditions for life to exist are too particular. Paragraph: _____

4 Answer the questions using the information in the text.

  1 How many solar systems are there in the universe?

    _____

  2 What is the name of the telescope that discovers new planets?

    _____

  3 What is Kepler 22b? _____

  4 Which university wrote a report saying that it is unlikely that there is life on other planets? _____

  5 What does the report say we need before we can know if there is life on other planets? _____

Kepler 22b

Life on Other Planets

1   For many years, people have **wondered** whether we are the only living things in the universe. Some scientists believe that there must be life on other planets because the universe is so big. However, it is **unlikely** that there is life on other planets because planets need a very specific environment for life to start. In the end, there are no facts that **support** the idea of life on other planets.

2   First of all, it is true that the universe is huge. It has billions of stars and thousands of solar systems. As of 2016, experts using the very powerful Kepler telescope[1] have found more than 2,300 planets in orbit around stars. A lot of these planets are similar to Earth. In fact, a number of scientists believe that one of these planets, named Kepler 22b, has the right **conditions**—the right atmosphere[2] and temperature—to support life. However, there is no **evidence** that there is life on Kepler 22b. Experts with the best technology can see no signs of life there. Until there is hard evidence, we cannot use Kepler 22b to support the idea of life on other planets.

3   A planet needs very **particular** conditions to support life. A planet with life would need to have water, the right temperature, and the right mix of chemicals in the atmosphere. Earth has the perfect conditions for life, and it is highly unlikely that another planet has exactly the same environment as Earth. In addition, although scientists believe that life might **exist** on other planets, they have never found evidence to **prove** it. A recent report from Princeton University suggests that it is highly unlikely that there is life on other planets. The researchers believe that we don't have enough scientific evidence to decide if there is life on other planets. They say that just because conditions similar to Earth exist on other planets, it doesn't mean that life exists there.

4   In conclusion, I do not believe that there is life on other planets. Although the universe is very big, a planet with life needs very special conditions. Earth has exactly the right conditions for life. It is not too hot or too cold. It has water, air, and the right chemicals. I do not think that any other planets could have exactly the same conditions as Earth. Therefore, I do not think that there could be life on other planets.

[1]**telescope** (n) a piece of equipment, in the shape of a tube, that makes things that are far away look bigger or nearer
[2]**atmosphere** (n) the layer of gases around a planet

READING BETWEEN THE LINES

5 Why do you think Kepler 22b was given its name?

6 Read the sentences from the text. Which are facts and which are opinions? Write *F* (fact) or *O* (opinion).

1 There must be life on other planets. _____
2 The universe has billions of stars and thousands of solar systems. _____
3 It is highly unlikely that there is life on other planets. _____
4 A planet needs very particular conditions to support life. _____

7 Read the questions and circle the correct answers.

1 What is the author's main purpose?
   a to entertain readers
   b to make readers agree with his or her opinion
   c to inform readers
2 What does the author believe?
   a The universe is so big that there must be life on other planets.
   b Life probably doesn't exist on other planets.
   c Life most likely exists on other planets; we just have to find it.
3 Why does the author include information from a recent report from Princeton University?
   a to prove that experts agree with his or her opinion
   b to show that there are two sides to the argument
   c to prove that life exists on other planets

DISCUSSION

8 Space exploration has led to many inventions. With a partner, rank these inventions in order of importance from *1* (the most important) to *7* (the least important).

a microcomputers _____   e electric cars _____
b GPS navigation _____   f robotic arms _____
c satellite TV _____   g freeze-dried food _____
d weather forecasts _____

9 Use information from Reading 1 and Reading 2 to answer the questions.

1 Will private companies make it possible for tourists to go to the moon or to explore planets like Mars or Kepler 22b? Why or why not?
2 Would private companies help us learn more about other planets and their environments? Why or why not?

GIVING EVIDENCE AND SUPPORTING AN ARGUMENT

In an essay, good writers support their arguments with evidence. The nouns *research, study, expert,* and *report* can be used to support arguments. Use the verbs *think* or *believe* for a person, and the verbs *show* or *suggest* for a piece of work.

PRISM Online Workbook

1 Write the nouns from the box next to the correct definitions. One definition has two correct answers.

> study   report   research   expert

1 _____ (n) someone who has a lot of skill in something or a lot of knowledge about something

2 _____ _____ (n) a document that tells us about a subject in detail

3 _____ (n) the study of a subject to discover new information

2 Complete the sentences with the correct verbs from the box. More than one answer is possible.

1 Experts _____ that the moon is too cold for people to live there.

2 Studies _____ that there are over 200 billion stars in the Milky Way galaxy.

3 Scientists _____ that we need to study space.

4 Reports _____ that parts of Mars were once covered in ice.

5 Research _____ that there could be 50 billion planets in our galaxy.

the Milky Way

WRITING

CRITICAL THINKING

At the end of this unit, you will complete an opinion essay. Look at this unit's Writing Task below.

> Should governments spend more money on space exploration?
> Give reasons and examples to support your opinion.

1 With a partner, look back at paragraph 1 of Reading 2 (page 177). What is the author's main argument?

_____

2 What are the reasons the author gives to support his or her argument? Look at paragraphs 2 and 3.

Paragraph 2: _____

_____

_____

_____

Paragraph 3: _____

_____

_____

_____

3 Read the opinions about funding for space exploration on page 181. Notice that the opinions come from different people and organizations. Underline the sentence or sentences that show the writer's opinion about funding space travel.

a

Source: The International Space Agency

Governments around the world should spend more money on space programs. The International Space Station (ISS) is a good example why. The ISS has existed since 1998 and brings together many countries. Astronauts live in space and take part in important experiments. In 2015, Russia and the U.S. sent astronauts to live on the ISS for one year to observe the effects of space on the human body. Long-term journeys, such as traveling to Mars, will never happen without this important research. The ISS cost about $100 billion, and one country could not pay for that on its own. International space exploration proves that countries can work together. It represents the spirit of partnership. With so much war in the world, governments should spend more money on things they can achieve together. Maybe that will help bring peace.

b

Source: A newspaper editorial

The U.S. has spent more than $16 billion per year on its space program since 1958. For a long time, the cost was worth it because of the advances made in science and technology. However, space travel is not only expensive, it is also dangerous. Astronauts have been killed as recently as 2014. Also, we shouldn't waste natural resources on building new spacecraft. More money should be spent on people who need clean water and food, access to education, and medical research. For example, a Japanese study found that a drug made from sea sponges helps treat several types of cancer. And yet 90% of the Earth's oceans are still unexplored. The ocean is a valuable resource. Governments should spend more money on ocean exploration than on space exploration.

c

Source: A government agency

Uncovering the mysteries of space is a huge task that should continue to be funded. Imagine the discoveries and advances in technology that will be made as countries go farther and farther into space, especially in the race to be the first to Mars. Furthermore, people may need to live on Mars someday because Earth will become too crowded and too hot. Also, asking questions about the universe encourages young people to study science and engineering, which is a huge benefit to society. Medical advances are also made as a result of sending humans to space. For example, when astronauts are in space, their bones become weaker and more likely to break. Many elderly people also have weak bones. Drugs that can help elderly people can be tested on astronauts in space. Research done in space can improve life on Earth. Governments should absolutely spend more money on space programs.

4 Complete the T-chart with the reasons and evidence the writers give for and against funding space exploration. List the source (a, b, or c) next to each reason you list.

for	against
Astronauts take part in important experiments (a)	

Evaluating arguments

It is important to think about how good the different arguments about a topic are. Some arguments are stronger than others. *Evaluate* by deciding how strong an argument is. Is there strong evidence to support the argument? Opinions must be supported by evidence (reasons and examples) to produce a valid argument. This can help you decide which arguments to include in an essay.

⯅ EVALUATE

5 Circle the arguments in the T-chart that are the most convincing. Then discuss with a partner why you think these arguments are the most convincing.

⯅ CREATE

6 Work with a partner. Think of evidence and examples for the arguments you chose in Exercise 5.

7 Which opinion do you agree with most? Explain why.

    a Governments should spend more money on exploring space.

    b Governments should not spend more money on exploring space.

GRAMMAR FOR WRITING

THAT CLAUSES IN COMPLEX SENTENCES

Good writers use a variety of sentence structures to make their writing interesting. Writers should use simple, compound, and complex sentences. In some complex sentences, *that* clauses are used to give supporting evidence.

That clauses begin with *that* and have their own subject and verb.

main clause		that clause	
subject	verb	subject	verb

NASA scientists learned **that human bones can become weaker in space**.

In conversation and informal writing, *that* is often omitted. In formal, academic writing, use *that*.

main clause		that clause	
subject	verb	subject	verb

Many people are sure **they will travel to Mars someday**. *(informal)*

main clause		that clause	
subject	verb	subject	verb

Many people are sure **that they will travel to Mars someday**. *(formal)*

You can use reporting verbs (*explain, think, show, say, believe, hope, doubt, claim, state, suggest*) in the main clause to give supporting evidence and examples for an argument. For example:

main clause

Some people think + *that* clause.
Studies show + *that* clause.
Scientists believe + *that* clause.
Some experts suggest + *that* clause.

There must be life on other planets. → **Some scientists believe** that there must be life on other planets.

1 Put the words in order to make complex sentences with *that* clauses.

1 we could live / by 2050 / on the moon / Scientists believe that / .

_____

2 not a planet / Reports show that / is / Pluto / .

_____

3 a good way / to learn about science / TV shows / are / Some people think that / .

_____

4 life / on other planets / Studies suggest that / could exist / .

_____

2 Rewrite the quotations as complex sentences with reporting verbs and *that* clauses.

1 "SpaceX built *Dragon* in order to deliver supplies to the International Space Station." –Elon Musk
Elon Musk said that SpaceX built *Dragon* in order to deliver supplies to the International Space Station.

2 "Regular people should have the opportunity to travel in space."
– Sir Richard Branson

3 "We doubt that alien life exists." – Researchers at Princeton University

4 "The Kepler telescope looks for livable planets beyond Earth." – NASA

INFINITIVES OF PURPOSE

You can use *in order to* + the base form of the verb to express a purpose, or why something is done. It answers a "Why?" question.

You can use *to* + the base form of the verb alone when the meaning is clear.
NASA sent robots to Mars **(in order) to find** water.
SpaceX designed *Dragon* **(in order) to deliver** supplies.

3 Match the sentence halves.

1 We build rockets
2 We sent the International Space Station into space
3 We want to land on the moon

a (in order) to explore it in more detail.
b (in order) to send people into space.
c (in order) to find out if people could live in space.

4 Complete the sentence in three different ways using infinitives.

1 We explore space (in order) _____ .
2 We explore space (in order) _____ .
3 We explore space (in order) _____ .

ACADEMIC WRITING SKILLS

ESSAY ORGANIZATION

An essay is a group of paragraphs about the same topic. Essays are common in academic writing. An essay responds to an essay question.

An essay has an *introductory paragraph*, one or more *main body paragraphs*, and a *concluding paragraph*.

Introductory paragraph: The introductory paragraph gives background information about a topic. Background information can be general information about the topic, historical information, or a story that helps readers understand why the topic is important. The last sentence of the introductory paragraph is the **thesis statement**. It tells the reader what the essay will be about. It is similar to a topic sentence for a paragraph, and it includes the writer's point of view. It also tells what the main body paragraphs will discuss.

Main body paragraphs: Each main body paragraph has a topic sentence and supporting sentences. Supporting sentences include facts, reasons, and examples that support the essay's ideas.

Concluding paragraph: The concluding paragraph retells or summarizes the main points in the essay. The writer gives his or her opinion again.

1 Use the words in the box to complete the summary about the correct order of paragraphs in an essay.

PRISM Online Workbook

| middle   last   first   one |

The introductory paragraph is the (1)_____ paragraph in an essay. The body is the (2)_____ paragraph or set of paragraphs of the essay. The body can be (3)_____ paragraph or many paragraphs. The concluding paragraph is the (4)_____ paragraph in an essay.

2 Look at the essay in Reading 2 again on page 177. Follow the instructions.

1 In the introductory paragraph, circle the background information about the topic. Underline the thesis statement.
2 In the body paragraphs, highlight the facts, reasons, and examples that support the argument.
3 In the concluding paragraph, circle the phrases that retell the main points in the essay. Underline the writer's opinion.

> Should governments spend more money on space exploration?
> Give reasons and examples to support your opinion.

PLAN

1 Look at the essay planner below and answer the questions.

    a In which paragraphs should you give support for your opinion?
    b In which paragraph should you write your conclusion?
    c In which paragraph should you include your opinion about the topic?
    d Should governments spend money on space exploration? Complete the thesis statement in the first paragraph of the essay planner. Then circle *should* or *should not* in the concluding paragraph to show your opinion.

2 Refer to the Task Checklist on page 187 as you prepare your essay.

WRITE A FIRST DRAFT

3 Use your ideas from Critical Thinking to complete the essay planner.

---

1   Space exploration is very expensive. Between 1981 and 2011, the U.S. government spent $192 billion on its space program. Many people believe that space exploration is a waste of money. However, other people think that it is an important and exciting project and that we should spend money on it. In my opinion, _____ _____ .

2 _____
_____
_____
_____
_____

3 _____
_____
_____
_____
_____

---

4   In conclusion, I think that governments should / should not spend money on space exploration. _____

_____

_____

_____

_____

REVISE

4 Use the Task Checklist to review your essay for content and structure.

TASK CHECKLIST	✔
Did you include arguments for or against governments spending money on space exploration?	
Did you write a thesis statement that tells what the essay is about and gives your point of view?	
Did you use evidence and examples to support your arguments?	
Did you summarize your main points and include your own opinion in the concluding paragraph?	

5 Make any necessary changes to your essay.

EDIT

6 Use the Language Checklist to edit your essay for language errors.

LANGUAGE CHECKLIST	✔
Did you use vocabulary to give evidence and support arguments?	
Did you use infinitives of purpose correctly?	
Did you use *that* clauses in complex sentences to give evidence and supporting details?	

7 Make any necessary changes to your essay.

ON CAMPUS

USING THE LIBRARY

SKILLS

Many students do a lot of their research on the Internet. But well-informed students also know that libraries and librarians are both great resources on college campuses.

PREPARING TO READ

1 Work with a partner. Discuss the questions.

1 How many libraries are there on your campus? How many of them have you visited?
2 Have you ever asked a librarian a question? Why or why not?
3 How often do you use the library for research?
4 What are some advantages of using a library instead of the Internet?

WHILE READING

2 Read a welcome page from a library website. Circle the answer to complete each sentence.

1 A database is a good resource for students because _____ .
   a they can trust the quality   b it is at the university
2 Google isn't a good tool for research because _____ .
   a it takes too long to find information b a database is better
3 Carol Klein says that reference librarians like to _____ .
   a do research at the library   b answer students' questions
4 When a student asks the librarian for help, he or she should _____ .
   a be specific   b know key words about the topic

3 Write T (true) or F (false) next to the statements.

_____ 1 Students should use databases instead of books for resources.
_____ 2 Archives are available for everyone online.
_____ 3 The most important thing is to start early on a research project.
_____ 4 Reference librarians want to help students with their research.
_____ 5 A student can find anything on the Internet.
_____ 6 Sometimes it's hard to find the name of the writer on the Internet.

Ford College
Library Resources

Welcome to Ford College. My name is Carol Klein. I am one of the reference librarians here on campus. Let me answer some common questions about the libraries and reference librarians.

What does a reference librarian do?

Reference librarians help people find information and resources in the library. They also teach students how to use the library and the databases[1] for their research. Students ask us questions about their research all day, and we love it. We are all here to help you!

Why should students use the library?

These days, many students use the Internet and Google to do their research, but Google is not a research tool. It can take you a long time to find the information you need. Also, on the Internet, you might not find important information, like who wrote an article or when the author wrote it.

There are many other reasons to use the library for your research:

- Reference librarians or resource assistants are available to help you find the best resources for projects and good key words[2] for searches.

- Not everything is on the Internet. You may need specialized resources, like old maps and newspapers, or archives[3]. Not all books are available online either, but they are excellent sources of information.

- College and university libraries have special databases for their students to use. They are organized so you can find information easily and quickly. The resources you find in these databases are controlled for quality, so they are always reliable[4].

What advice do you have for students?

- Start your research early.
- Don't be afraid to ask questions.
- Be specific when you ask for help. Tell the librarian your topic, your assignment, and any questions you have.

Come visit us!

[1]**database** (n) a collection of information or articles that is organized so it is easy to use
[2]**key words** (n) important words about a topic for searching for information
[3]**archives** (n) collections of historic documents
[4]**reliable** (adj) able to be trusted; dependable

PRACTICE

4 Work with a partner. Choose a topic from this book that you want to know more about. Write two questions you can ask a reference librarian about your topic. Ask about a fact, and then ask about resources.

REAL-WORLD APPLICATION

5 Work with the same partner. Follow the steps to research the topic you chose in Exercise 4.

1 Go to the library. Introduce yourself to a reference librarian.
2 Tell the librarian about your topic and ask your questions.
3 Ask the librarian for two good key words for your topic.
4 Ask the librarian if the library has the following items:
   databases   maps   newspapers   archives

6 Share your information with the class.

GLOSSARY OF KEY VOCABULARY

Words that are part of the Academic Word List are noted with an **A** in this glossary.

UNIT 1 PLACES

READING 1

capital (n) the most important city in a country or state; where the government is

countryside (n) land that is not in towns or cities and may have farms and fields

expert **A** (n) someone who has a lot of skill in or a lot of knowledge about something

modern (adj) designed and made using the most recent ideas and methods

opportunity (n) a chance to do or experience something good

pollution (n) damage caused to water, air, and land by harmful materials or waste

population (n) the number of people living in a place

traffic (n) the cars, trucks, and other vehicles using a road

READING 2

area **A** (n) a region or part of a larger place, like a country or city

cheap (adj) not expensive, or costs less than usual

downtown (adj) the main or central part of a city

expensive (adj) costs a lot of money; not cheap

local (adj) relating to a particular area, city, or town

noisy (adj) loud; makes a lot of noise

quiet (adj) makes little or no noise

UNIT 2 FESTIVALS AND CELEBRATIONS

READING 1

celebrate (v) to do something enjoyable because it is a special day

culture **A** (n) the habits, traditions, and beliefs of a country or group of people

gift (n) something that you give to someone, usually on a special day

the ground (n) the surface of the Earth

lucky (adj) having good things happen to you

traditional **A** (adj) following the ways of behaving or doing things that have continued in a group of people for a long time

READING 2

activity (n) something people do for fun

highlight **A** (n) the most enjoyable part of something

history (n) the whole series of events in the past that relate to the development of a country, subject, or person

popular (adj) liked by many people

take part in (phr v) to do an activity with other people

visitor (n) someone who goes to see a person or a place

UNIT 3 THE INTERNET AND TECHNOLOGY

READING 1

benefit Ⓐ (n) a good or helpful result or effect

collect (v) to get things from different places and bring them together

free (adj) costing no money

interest (n) something you enjoy doing or learning about

record (v) to store sounds, pictures, or information on a camera or computer so that they can be used in the future

secret (adj) not known or seen by other people

security Ⓐ (n) the things that are done to keep someone or something safe

software (n) programs you use to make a computer do different things

READING 2

affect Ⓐ (v) to influence someone or something; to cause change

creative Ⓐ (adj) good at thinking of new ideas or creating new and unusual things

download (v) to copy computer programs, music, or other information electronically from the Internet to your computer

educational (adj) providing education, or relating to education

imagination (n) the part of your mind that creates ideas or pictures of things that are not real or that you have not seen

improve (v) to get better or to make something better

UNIT 4 WEATHER AND CLIMATE

READING 1

almost (adv) not everything, but very close to it

cover (v) to lie on the surface of something

dangerous (adj) can harm or hurt someone or something

huge (adj) extremely large in size or amount

last (v) to continue for a period of time

lightning (n) a flash of bright light in the sky during a storm

thunder (n) the sudden loud noise that comes after a flash of lightning

READING 2

careful (adj) paying attention to what you are doing so that you do not have an accident, make a mistake, or damage something

decide (v) to choose between one possibility or another

drop (v) to decrease; to fall or go down

precipitation (n) rain or snow that falls to the ground

rise (v) to increase; to go up

shock (n) a big, unpleasant surprise

UNIT 5 SPORTS AND COMPETITION

READING 1

ancient (adj) from a long time ago; very old

compete (v) to take part in a race or competition; to try to be more successful than someone else

competition (n) an organized event in which people try to win a prize by being the best

strange (adj) not familiar; difficult to understand; different

swimming (n) a sport where people move through water by moving their body

take place (phr v) to happen

throw (v) to send something through the air, pushing it out of your hand

READING 2

accident (n) something bad that happens that is not intended and that causes injury or damage

challenging Ⓐ (adj) difficult in a way that tests your ability

climb (v) to go up something or onto the top of something, like a tree or mountain

course (n) an area used for sports events, such as racing or playing golf

in shape (adj) in good health; strong

participant Ⓐ (n) someone who takes part in an activity

UNIT 6 BUSINESS

READING 1

apply (v) to ask officially for something, often by writing

colleague Ⓐ (n) someone that you work with

customer (n) someone who buys things from a store or business

occupation Ⓐ (n) a job or career

organize (v) to plan or arrange carefully

result (n) information that you find out from something, such as an exam, a scientific experiment, or a medical test

READING 2

advertise (v) to tell people about a product or service, for example in newspapers or on television, in order to persuade them to buy it

employ (v) to pay someone to work or do a job for you

goal Ⓐ (n) something you want to do successfully in the future

introduce (v) to make something available to buy or use for the first time

office (n) a place in a building where people work

partner (n) someone who runs or owns a business with another person

run (v) to manage or operate something

set up (phr v) to create or establish (something) for a particular purpose

UNIT 7 PEOPLE

READING 1

blind (adj) not able to see

incredible (adj) impossible or very difficult to believe; amazing

inspire (v) to make other people feel that they want to do something

operation (n) the process when doctors cut your body to repair it or to take something out

respect (v) to like or to have a very good opinion of someone because of their knowledge, achievements, etc.

talent (n) a natural ability to do something well

READING 2

achieve Ⓐ (v) to succeed in doing something difficult

brave (adj) not afraid of dangerous or difficult situations

dream (n) something that you really want to do, be, or have in the future

former (adj) before the present time or in the past

honest (adj) truthful or able to be trusted; not likely to lie, cheat, or steal

intelligent Ⓐ (adj) able to learn and understand things easily; smart

take care of (phr v) to care for or be responsible for someone or something

train (v) to prepare for a job, activity, or sport by learning skills or by exercise

UNIT 8 THE UNIVERSE

READING 1

advance (n) progress in the development or improvement of something

beyond (prep) on the farther side of; at a farther distance than

crash (v) to hit something by accident, especially in a vehicle

entrepreneur (n) someone who starts their own business

explore (v) to travel to a new place to learn about it

private (adj) related to money or services controlled or supplied by a person or a company and not by the government

public (adj) related to money or services controlled or supplied by the government and not by a person or a company

READING 2

condition (n) the physical state that someone or something is in

evidence Ⓐ (n) something that makes you believe something is true

exist (v) to be real, alive, or present

particular (adj) used to talk about one thing or person and not others

prove (v) to show that something is true

support (v) to help show that something is true

unlikely (adj) not expected to happen; not probable

wonder (v) to think about something and try to understand it

VIDEO SCRIPTS

UNIT 1

▶ The Top U.S. City

Reporter: Called the Holy City, for its many church steeples, peaked above the city's low-slung skyline, it beat out San Francisco, which had won the award 18 years in a row. I think people, at times, are surprised to hear that. Charleston Mayor, Joe Riley.

Joe Riley: Well, you know, when people come to Charleston, whether they're from the U.S. or from another continent, for the first time, they're always surprised. It's like they didn't know this kind of place existed in America.

Reporter: Charleston was a cradle of the Confederacy. It was here the first shots of the Civil War were fired. That history can be felt all around, from streets paved in stones, once used as ballast in sailing ships, to centuries-old houses that line the battery, to the city market, where vendors still sell their handmade crafts. And that doesn't even touch on the great southern cuisine. These are the draws for visitors to Charleston, where the thrill rides don't occur on twisting scream machines, but rather on more sedate vehicles.

Joe Riley: We regulate very carefully the tourism industry. We regulate the number of carriages, where they go. We regulate where buses can go. We regulate the size of walking tours.

Reporter: All that attention to tourism is because it's big business here. 4 million visitors pump more than 3 billion dollars a year into the local economy.

Tom Doyle: Here we go.

Reporter: Tom Doyle has been leading carriage tours in Charleston for more than 30 years.
The attention that Charleston is getting right now, does that surprise you?

Tom Doyle: Uh, no, it doesn't. It surprises me it took as long as it did.
You can go down any street here, look to your left and look to your right and see even more beautiful streets. You can make Charleston your own special place.
Isn't this a great city?

Reporter: It's beautiful, I have to say.

UNIT 2

▶ The Meaning of Independence Day

Reporter: To kick off your Fourth of July celebration, how 'bout a little trip to Philadelphia, home of the Second Continental Congress. We found some young Americans in Philly who are learning about the nation's early days from some rather familiar faces.

Men: We hold these truths to be self-evident, that all men are created equal.

Man 1: The Fourth of July is very significant. It is the date upon which we approved the Declaration of Independence.

Woman: I believe that it symbolizes the great unity of our colonies, our collective effort to create our own constellation, our own country.

Young man 1: I think of collaboration, I think of, uh, kind of the best of America, where people—well, the delegates debated together and they really wanted to send a strong message to Britain.
It's really—you know, it's a great day to be American.

Boy 1: Well, I like all the fireworks, and all that's really fun and stuff.

Girl 1: Fireworks.

Girl 2: Our neighbors, like, buy like whole entire box of fireworks, and then they take them and they put them by the sewer and they light them.

Boy 2: Well, the fireworks and it's really fun, but it's like remembering all the people that laid down their lives for us.

Young woman: And I think it's such an important day for us as a nation to celebrate and remember every year. And I think it's so uniting too, to really remember what we were founded on and how blessed we are as a nation.

Young man 2: The sacrifice it took to make this nation and the opportunity we have that many people around the world don't have to life, liberty, and the pursuit of happiness. It's really a neat opportunity to remember how blessed we are to be in this country.

UNIT 3

▶ Predictive Advertising

Narrator: Every time we make a phone call, search online, or buy something, we leave information, or data, about our habits. And the amount of data is getting bigger by 2.5 billion gigabytes every day. All that data is worth a lot of money.

Mike Baker is a "data hunter." He collects data. He thinks this information is changing the way we live and the way we do business.

A few years ago, Mike decided to help advertisers. Why should companies wait for people to find their ads when it was now possible to bring personalized ads to everyone?

Then he had another idea. If companies had enough information about people's past activities, could they use this information to predict their future activities?

Mike felt that they could—that they could predict what people might want to buy. But it was difficult because there was too much data. He needed a program to understand and use the data.

And he wanted to be able to use the data fast—to be able to predict what people wanted to buy, before they even knew it. But he needed help.

So Mike found a partner with a superfast program. Together, they made the program do what Mike wanted it to do. The program looks at data very quickly and finds clues about what people might want to buy.

Then it sends them personalized ads. For example, it might learn that you like Italian food and are interested in cars, so it sends you ads about those things.

We now live in a world of personalized ads. Yes, you can choose not to have personalized ads, but you can't get away from ads completely. So maybe it's better to see ads for things you like than for things you don't care about.

UNIT 4

▶ Tornadoes

Narrator: In the middle of the United States, spring brings warm, wet air from the south, making things perfect for one of the most extreme weather events on Earth—tornadoes. That's why this part of the country is called Tornado Alley.

Some years are worse than others, and 2011 was one of the worst ever.

Man: Did you see that? The whole house came apart! Oh my God! Oh my God!

Narrator: That year, in the town of Joplin, Missouri, a dangerous tornado killed more than 160 people.

But although we know a lot about the science of tornadoes, we still can't predict exactly when or where they will happen.

Josh Wurman is a weather scientist. He and his team are studying how thunderstorms produce tornadoes.

Seventy-five percent of thunderstorms don't produce tornadoes, but twenty-five percent of them do. But which thunderstorms will do it? To answer this question, Josh and his team need to get information from as many tornadoes as they can during the spring. To find the storms, Josh uses a Doppler radar scanner. It can show him what's going on inside a thunderstorm, which gives him important information about what starts a tornado.

Josh now knows where to look, but finding the right storm is always difficult. Then, after 1,000 miles of driving, they find the right one. But the team has to move fast because tornadoes come and go very quickly.

And there's the tornado they're looking for.

Woman: There we go. That's what it's about.

Man 1: Yeah.

Man 2: There she is.

Man 1: It's a beauty.

Man 2: It's a beauty.

Man on radio: Be careful. Be careful.

Narrator: This huge tornado is less than a mile away from the team.

Its winds are spinning up to 200 miles per hour.

But less than 30 minutes after the tornado appeared, it dies. It was one of more than 1,200 tornadoes in this part of Tornado Alley since the beginning of spring.

UNIT 5

▶ Skiing in the French Alps

Narrator: This is Courchevel, France. It's popular with skiers. There are four villages, and the names tell you the height in meters, like Courchevel 1,300 and Courchevel 1,850, which is the highest most well-known. Rich and famous people, like the American movie star Leonardo DiCaprio, ski here.

In slalom skiing, skiers race between the red and blue flags. The slalom course is in the highest village. Emma Carrick-Anderson is a British skier. She competed in the Winter Olympics.

Dallas Campbell isn't an Olympic skier. But he's ready to race.

Ski official: Left course ready, right course ready, and go!

Narrator: In an Olympic race, the difference between first and tenth place is often less than one second.

We're going to see how to prepare skis to make them go as fast as possible in the snow.

First, they "grind" the bottom of the skis to make them smooth.

Next, they use a special wax to fill in the holes. Then, they make the skis smooth again.

Now his skis are prepared, and Dallas is ready to race Emma again.

Ski official: Yeah, go.

Dallas Campbell: Ah-ha. Ah.

UNIT 6

▶ Amazon's Fulfillment Center

Narrator: Today Amazon is the world's largest online store. But its first warehouse was a small basement in Seattle, Washington.

Now, with more than 100 million items for sale on its website, Amazon has many large warehouses around the world called "fulfillment centers." How do they find your item? Only the central computer knows where everything is. Any item can be on any shelf. In fact, their location is random so that workers don't take the wrong item.

After you order and pay for an item online, an Amazon worker walks through the warehouse and finds your kitchen item or your cute toy. The computer then tells the workers the right size of the box.

Finally, your name and address goes on the box before it leaves the fulfillment center.

UNIT 7

▶ The 101-Year-Old Weather Volunteer

Reporter: Across the country, 8,500 volunteer observers record the nation's weather every day, but none has been doing it longer than 101-year-old Richard Hendrickson.

Richard: Right now, it is exactly 80.

Reporter: For 84 years now, Hendrickson's been monitoring the highs and lows from the thermometer shelter in his backyard in Bridgehampton, New York.

Is this pretty much the way it's always been?

Richard: Oh, yeah.

Reporter: Real simple.

Richard: Just like that. You're getting to show age a little bit here in the joints.

Reporter: We all do.

Richard: Like we all get.

Reporter: He also checks the rainfall daily. And then glances out his dining room window to check the wind.

Richard: It's clear. There's not a cloud in the sky.

Reporter: Before calling it all in on his rotary phone ...

Richard: Yeah, Bridgehampton.

Reporter: ... to the National Weather Service.

Richard: The sky is clear. The wind is out of the southwest.

Reporter: When Hendrickson started recording the weather in 1930, at age 18, Herbert Hoover was president.

This is your journal from the '30s.

Richard: Sure I remember this thing. I'll be damned. In 1933. January. Clear and warm.

Reporter: Weather was important to you because you were a farmer.

Richard: Because I was a livestock farmer.

Reporter: This weekend, the National Weather Service will honor his eight decades as an observer.

Richard: Am I what? Excited? Oh, yeah, sure. I can hardly talk.

Reporter: He does it for his country, Richard Hendrickson says. Collecting the statistics that to this 101-year-old farmer are still just the facts of life.

UNIT 8

▶ Going to the International Space Station

Narrator: Most people drive or take a bus, train, or subway to work.

But Sunita Williams is different.

Every morning she gets up, takes her dog for a walk, and gets ready for work. But sometimes when she goes to work, her vehicle is very unusual. Yes, it takes her 15–20 minutes with traffic to drive her car two miles to the office in Houston, Texas.

But we're not talking about that vehicle or that office.

She has a special vehicle she takes to a different office, and traffic's not a problem.

Captain Sunita Williams is an American astronaut. In 2012 she spent four months in a very special office—the International Space Station.

She traveled to the space station in this Russian Soyuz rocket.

The trip was 250 miles, straight up.

The trip to space took just nine minutes. That's half the time it usually takes Sunita to drive to work.

Sunita Williams traveled in a tiny capsule on top of hundreds of tons of rocket power.

After she, Russian cosmonaut Yuri Malenchenko, and Japanese astronaut Akihiko Hoshide climbed the stairs and rode the elevator to the top, they went inside. Then it was time to blast off for the International Space Station.

Man: T-minus ten, nine, eight, seven, six, five, four, three, two, one.

Lift off. Lift off of the Soyuz TMA05M, carrying Suni Williams, Yuri Malenchenko, and Aki Hoshide on a journey to the International Space Station.

The authors and publishers acknowledge the following sources of copyright material and are grateful for the permissions granted. While every effort has been made, it has not always been possible to identify the sources of all the material used, or to trace all copyright holders. If any omissions are brought to our notice, we will be happy to include the appropriate acknowledgements on reprinting and in the next update to the digital edition, as applicable.

Text credits

Graphs on p. 92 adapted from 'Anchorage Climate Graph – Alaska Climate Chart'. Copyright © US Climate Data; Graphs on p. 93 adapted from 'Amman, Amman Governorate Monthly Climate Average, Jordan'. Copyright © worldweatheronline. Reproduced with kind permission.

Photo credits

Key: T = Top, C = Center, B = Below, L = Left, R = Right, BG = Background.

p. 12: Cultura RM Exclusive/Peter Muller/Getty Images; pp. 14–15: Danita Delimont/Gallo Images/Getty Images; p. 23 (T): Andrew Bret Wallis/The Image Bank/Getty Images; p. 23 (B): Zubin Shroff/The Image Bank/Getty Images; p. 26: Roberto Machado Noa/LightRocket; p. 30: Joseph Plotz/Moment Open/Getty Images; pp. 36–37: epa european pressphoto agency b.v./Alamy; p. 37 (L): Per-Andre Hoffmann/LOOK-foto/Getty Images; p. 37 (C): Rich-Joseph Facun/arabianEye/Getty Images; p. 37 (R): Robyn Breen Shinn/Cultura Exclusive/Getty Images; p. 41 (pinatas): Sollina Images/The Image Bank/Getty Images; p. 41 (noodles): Chia Hsien Lee/EyeEm/Getty Images; p. 41 (mother's day): ONOKY - Fabrice LEROUGE/Brand X Pictures/Getty Images; p. 41 (name days): Christopher Kimmel/Moment/Getty Images; p. 41 (women): Andia/Universal Images Group/Getty Images; p. 43: Richard I'Anson/Lonely Planet Images/Getty Images; p. 44 (T): Marwan Naamani/AFP/Getty Images; p. 44 (B): John Elk/Lonely Planet Images/Getty Images; pp. 58–59: R. Hamilton Smith/Passage/Getty Images; p. 63 (L): Kelvin Murray/Taxi/Getty Images; p. 63 (R): andresr/E+/Getty Images; pp. 80–81: WIN-Initiative/Getty Images; p. 81 (photo 1): Bryan Mullennix/The Image Bank/Getty Images; p. 81 (photo 2): Ariadne Van Zandbergen/Lonely Planet Images/Getty Images; p. 81 (photo 3): BOISVIEUX Christophe/hemis.fr/Getty Images; p. 81 (photo 4): Andre Gallant/Photographer's Choice/Getty Images; pp. 102–103: Eric Estrade/AFP/Getty Images; p. 107: Colin McConnell/Toronto Star/Getty Images; p. 108 (L): Peter Parks/AFP/Getty Images; p. 108 (R): Andrew Pickett/Britain On View/Getty Images; p. 112: Mike Hewitt/Getty Images Sport/Getty Images; p. 123: Hero Images/Getty Images; pp. 124–125: Pavel L Photo and Video/Shutterstock; p. 125 (T): Chesnot/Getty Images News/Getty Images; p. 125 (B): David Ramos/Getty Images News/Getty Images; p. 133: Justin Sullivan/Getty Images News/Getty Images; p. 144 (T): William King/The Image Bank/Getty Images; p. 144 (B): Campus Life/Getty Images; p. 145 : Westend61/Getty Images; pp. 146–147: Tom Bonaventure/Getty Images; p. 147 (L), p. 155 (T): Sean Gallup/Getty Images News/Getty Images; p. 147 (C): Tim Graham/Tim Graham Photo Library/Getty Images; p. 147 (R): Ullstein Bild/Getty Images; p. 151: Sacramento Bee/Tribune News Service/Getty Images; p. 155 (B): Sean Drakes/CON/LatinContent Editorial/Getty Images; p. 163: AFP/Getty Images; pp. 168–169: NASA/VRS/Science Photo Library; p. 173 (T): Robyn Beck/AFP/Getty Images; p. 173 (B): Bloomberg/Getty Images; p. 176: Stocktrek Images/Getty Images; p. 179: Inigo Cia/Moment/Getty Images.

Front cover photographs by (man) SharpPhoto/Shutterstock and (BG) PlusONE/Shutterstock.

Illustrations

by Ben Hasler (NB Illustration) p. 112 (nettle) and p. 118; Fiona Gowen p. 112 (map), pp. 114–115.

Video Supplied by BBC Worldwide Learning.

Video Stills Supplied by BBC Worldwide Learning.

Corpus

Development of this publication has made use of the Cambridge English Corpus (CEC). The CEC is a multi-billion word computer database of contemporary spoken and written English. It includes British English, American English, and other varieties of English. It also includes the Cambridge Learner Corpus, developed in collaboration with the University of Cambridge ESOL Examinations. Cambridge University Press has built up the CEC to provide evidence about language use that helps to produce better language teaching materials

Cambridge Dictionaries

Cambridge dictionaries are the world's most widely used dictionaries for learners of English. The dictionaries are available in print and online at dictionary.cambridge.org. Copyright © Cambridge University Press, reproduced with permission.

Typeset by emc design ltd.

INFORMED BY TEACHERS

Classroom teachers shaped everything about *Prism*. The topics. The exercises. The critical thinking skills. The On Campus sections. Everything. We are confident that *Prism* will help your students succeed in college because teachers just like you helped guide the creation of this series.

Prism Advisory Panel

The members of the *Prism* Advisory Panel provided inspiration, ideas, and feedback on many aspects of the series. *Prism* is stronger because of their contributions.

Gloria Munson
University of Texas, Arlington

Kim Oliver
Austin Community College

Gregory Wayne
Portland State University

Julaine Rosner
Mission College

Dinorah Sapp
University of Mississippi

Christine Hagan
George Brown College/Seneca College

Heidi Lieb
Bergen Community College

Stephanie Kasuboski
Cuyahoga Community College

Global Input

Teachers from more than 500 institutions all over the world provided valuable input through:
- Surveys
- Focus Groups
- Reviews